THINKING
ABOUT
ABORTION

Books by Beryl Lieff Benderly

DANCING WITHOUT MUSIC: DEAFNESS IN AMERICA

DISCOVERING CULTURE: AN INTRODUCTION TO
ANTHROPOLOGY (Coauthor)

BERYL LIEFF BENDERLY

THINKING
ABOUT
ABORTION

The Dial Press
Doubleday & Co., Inc.
Garden City, N.Y.

1984

Library of Congress Cataloging in Publication Data

Benderly, Beryl Lieff.
  Thinking about abortion.

  Bibliography: p. 185
  Includes index.
  1. Abortion. I. Title.
RG734.B55 1984   613.9   83–45243
ISBN 0-385-27757-1

Published by The Dial Press

First printing

To the memory of my friend
Harriet Bisgaier Burg
a model of courage and humanity

PREFACE

Most of the people who helped me with this book cannot be thanked by name. This is more than an interesting coincidence; it is a significant comment on the nature of abortion in America. Not that I had any difficulty finding women (and sometimes men) eager to share their experiences with abortion. Wherever I went, in the unlikeliest places, people who learned of my project would make themselves known. They'd sidle over quietly at meetings, or stay at parties after others had gone, or call on the phone the next day. "Maybe," they'd say solemnly, "you'd like to talk with *me.*" People I knew socially, people I knew professionally, people I had just met, and people I had known for years all came forward with the stories that illumine this book. Some had never spoken of their experiences with anyone before, but all recounted their tales with clarity and feeling. They gave me everything I needed—except the permission to name them in public. But they know who they are, and I do sincerely thank them one and all.

There are, fortunately, others whose contributions I can acknowledge publicly. Nancy Warford, R.N., and her staff at the Northern Virginia Women's Medical Center; Barbara Radford, M.S., of the Pre-Term clinic in Washington, D.C.; Marjorie Deutsch, Ph.D.; Susan Pasco, R.N.; Dr. Curtis Boyd and Glenna Boyd of the Fairmount Center in Dallas, Texas; and Alice White of the National Abortion Federation provided information and insights that made this book possible. Mary Evans, as always, was a tireless friend in need. And my husband and children once again cheerfully tolerated the chancy temperament and erratic schedule of a wife and mother with a book on her mind.

I'd also like to thank an institution that by now seems a personal friend. The National Library of Medicine, one of the world's great scholarly resources, provided its usual speedy, helpful service, comfortable surroundings; and a seemingly inexhaustible supply of books and articles.

My friend Harriet Burg, a lawyer deeply interested in legal issues relating to women and to health, also helped on this project, as she had in the past, with sound advice on sources; constant, bracing encouragement; and thoughtful discussion of complicated issues. Tragically, though, she did not live to see the result of these efforts. In the hope that this book might, in some small way, honor that dauntless and compassionate spirit, I fondly dedicate it to her memory.

B.L.B.
August 1983

CONTENTS

THINKING
ABOUT
ABORTION

1/

FIRST THINGS

"The night my father got me his mind was not on me."

A. E. Housman

Few people who've had anything to do with an abortion ever forget it. Whether they fathered the pregnancy, sat up with an anguished friend, or themselves lay down on the doctor's table, they will hold that day, and incidents in the days leading up to it, etched with the harsh clarity reserved for only the most momentous memories. The look of an unfamiliar room, the sound of a stranger's voice, the small details of a day unlike any other may stay with them forever after. But the road to an abortion usually begins quite offhandedly, in some well-known and comfortable place, on a day or night like many others.

People rarely understand at the time that they've started out on a forced march down a road with few exits; an unwanted pregnancy is an involuntary trip that must end up somewhere people don't want to be, as either the parent of a new baby or a participant in an abortion. But since this journey leads to all the rest of their lives, it would help if they knew the landmarks.

And, it surprises many to learn, there are pretty well-established milestones. Although an extraordinary calamity in any particular life, an unwanted pregnancy is a commonplace in our country at large, and abortion is very close to being that too. Thousands upon thousands of women and men, therefore, travel this same road, struggle with the same thoughts and feelings, pass through the same set of obstacles, and arrive at one of the very few possible destinations. But most individuals and couples feel intensely that they have essentially traveled alone.

Abortion is at once the simplest and most complex surgical procedure commonly performed today. From a strictly technical standpoint, a routine first-trimester vacuum aspiration wouldn't tax the skills of a well-trained paramedic. But in its emotional, moral, and social aspects, the question of abortion has engaged the passionate interest of psychiatrists, theologians, politicians, and philosophers. Though less painful than a tooth extraction and safer than a tonsillectomy, the procedure has been debated and studied like no other. And still it lies at the center of both a profound national debate about the social order and of many women's deepest considerations about their own natures.

In 1973 the Supreme Court placed the decision to end a pregnancy, like that to remove a wart or straighten a nose, in the hands of the patient and her doctor. But, in the words of Dr. Bernard Nathanson, a deeply thoughtful former abortionist, "abortion is no more a medical issue because doctors do it than capital punishment is a matter of electrical engineering because an electric chair is used."[1]

Others who've studied the experience of abortion heartily agree. Although a surgical operation figures centrally, the purely medical questions are generally almost trivial. The real question is one that no amount of medical knowledge can answer: What should this woman do about the fetus growing inexorably inside her? The answer depends on what the woman believes to be true about herself, about those around her, and about her entire world. Finding the answer means exploring and often altering those beliefs.

But, as we've said, the road to abortion begins innocently, or at least unconsciously, enough. A woman conceives and then, at some point after discovering this fact, decides that she does not wish to carry the pregnancy to term. In a small number of the saddest cases irreversible genetic or other damage convinces a couple to abort a wanted—often deeply desired—pregnancy. But in the commonest American case a woman conceives without meaning to and then aborts for reasons far more related to social circumstances than to health.

The news that she's pregnant may not surprise her, but it nonetheless often comes as a terrific shock. "I kind of knew I had to be pregnant," says a woman we'll call Paula, recalling her college days, "but when the doctor told me, I couldn't believe it." Mary K. Zimmerman, a sociologist who conducted one of the few existing systematic studies of the experience of abortion in America, finds this apparently paradoxical reaction not only typical but highly significant.

To become pregnant, of course, a woman like Paula must engage in sexual intercourse. To discover that she's pregnant she must observe certain changes in her body that she knows can indicate the pregnant state; she may even test her suspicions with a drugstore test kit. To confirm the pregnancy means a trip to a doctor's office, laboratory, or clinic; then analysis of a urine sample; and, finally, a phone call or conversation bearing the welcome or unwelcome news. In their conscious minds, therefore, most women who have missed a menstrual period or two, noticed weight gain or tenderness of the breasts, experienced unexplained nausea and fatigue, and arranged a test already have considered the possibility, even probability, of pregnancy. But, still, among the forty abortion veterans she interviewed at great length, Zimmerman writes, many of the women "were shocked upon actually hearing what they expected to hear."[2]

That they still registered shock reflects the stigma they attached to pregnancy. It is difficult to accept deviance in oneself. The same kind of denial that had led them to ignore the possibility of pregnancy while they engaged in unprotected intercourse influenced their recognition of pregnancy once it occurred.[3]

"It just can't be," women say. Or "How can this happen to *me?*" Or, simply, "It's not possible."

If, like Paula, a woman is not married, discovering the pregnancy can mean not only finding herself in an unpleasant fix but having gotten there by doing or being something she theoretically shouldn't have. Even many of the married women are also guilty in their own eyes, at least of being inadequate contraceptors. "How could I, with all my experience, have been so dumb?" asks Liz, a wife of nearly fifteen years and mother of her desired number of planned children, with a rueful laugh.

The fact of unwanted pregnancy therefore imparts two unwelcome bits of information: one about the body and one about one's character. "I didn't think I was the sort of person this happened to," says Ellen. For Zimmerman the experience of the next several weeks—what she calls the "passage through abortion"—involves coping with these two pieces of news.

On one level handling the situation means deciding what to do or not do about the inescapable fact that unless action is taken a birth will almost certainly occur in seven or eight months. But on another, and to Zimmerman the more important, level, handling the situation means coming to terms with some other inescapable facts: One is either capable or incapable of having an abortion or capable or incapable of bearing an illegitimate or deeply unwanted child. "It took me a while to get used to the idea of what I was thinking of doing," Ellen says.

The fact of pregnancy is, obviously, much more than a physical fact. The birth of a child always entails a change, and sometimes a very drastic one, in a woman's circumstances. If a first birth, it causes possibly the most drastic social role shift possible in a woman's life: It makes her a mother. And, like other drastic role changes, it doesn't happen all at once. Indeed, women's perceptions of their pregnancies alter over time, passing through three phases: " 'My period is late'; 'I am pregnant'; 'I am going to have a baby.' "[4]

American women live in a country that permits cheap and easy access to early abortion, so the possibility of terminating an unwanted pregnancy always exists, at least in theory. But despite ease, cheapness, and legal legitimacy for over a decade, abortion still lacks full moral legitimacy for most people, including even many who advocate its availability. "When I meet people at a party or somewhere, I don't volunteer where I work," says the director of an abortion clinic. "If they ask me, I'll tell the name. Then they say, 'That's an abortion clinic, isn't it?' You can never tell how someone will react, and I get some very odd looks sometimes."

Though perfectly legal, abortion still strikes many as at least a bit shady; the reek of the back alley and the coat hanger still cling to the idea. Thus, our society sends women a very ambiguous signal; the act is legal but maybe not quite the proper thing to do. So, even considering such an act has a very ambiguous meaning for many women. It's her right to go ahead, but a truly nice girl wouldn't.

This ambiguity expresses itself in something no reader of the small body of existing literature on the experience (as opposed to the morality) of abortion can fail to note: the almost obsessive interest in confidentiality. In articles, reports, and books (including this one) authors disguise personal identities, names and features of clinics, even regions of the country. Every interviewer alters any possible indentifying evidence. Why should so many people be so loathe to talk for attribution about one of the most memorable experiences of their lives, an event that was fully legal and executed by one of society's premier symbols of respectability, a doctor of medicine? This fear of exposure goes beyond the reticence normal in talking about sex, or the embarrassment entailed by being caught red-handed in any other awkward, foolish mistake. The reason people say, "I wouldn't want my parents to find out" or "I never told anyone before" is because, Zimmerman writes, most women entering their own abortion passage believed the act (or possibly even the intention) "represented a form of deviance."[5] Dealing with that belief proved to be the crux of the entire experience for the women she studied.

Beyond its psychological interest, furthermore, this widespread perception of abortion as deviant remarkably illuminates the true issues at stake in the national controversy. The dictionary defines "deviant" as "differing from a norm or from the standard practice of a society." Although abortion may indeed differ from a norm, in the sense of an ideal of behavior, it has always been a standard practice of American society. As far back as records exist, even throughout the ninety years of criminalization, abortion has been common in America. In a landmark 1936 study Frederick J. Taussig placed the number at more than half a million abortions annually. In the 1950s Alfred Kinsey's studies of ordinary Middle Western women found that over 90 percent of premarital pregnancies ended in abortion; furthermore, 22 percent of his respondents admitted to having aborted *after* marriage.[6] A publication of Kinsey's Institute for Sex Research reported in 1958 that 7,074 ordinary American women admitted to a total of 1,067 induced abortions.[7] Indeed, the authors concluded, "It was found that induced abortion of a premarital pregnancy was a fairly common event" and, further, that "the great majority of all induced abortion stems from pregnancy in marriage."[8]

This from deep in the heart of the country and deep in the Eisenhower years. The true number of abortions performed in America before legalization can never be known, but most authorities accept Taussig's estimate as certainly reliable and possibly conservative. With legalization demographers have counted more carefully; abortions now approach a million and a half a year, but experts do not agree on what percentage of this number represents a true increase over prelegalization days and what percentage more accurate reporting. At any rate, abortion is now known to be the first or second most common surgical procedure performed in the United States.

With at least a half million operations a year, year after year for generations, there are at least twenty or thirty million living American women who have had abortions. People's mothers, grandmothers, aunts, neighbors, sisters, daughters, and best friends have had them. Between 1967 and 1979 fully "15% of U.S. women of reproductive age had legal abortions,"[9] and six of those years precede full national legalization. Malcolm Potts, Peter Diggory, and John Peel state, in their authoritative 1977 book *Abortion*, that "over the past five years almost one in five of New York women of reproductive age has had an abortion."[10]

And yet, with all those millions of women, with all those millions of experiences all around them, Zimmerman's subjects and many other women each still experience themselves as deviant and alone. "Women seeking abortions are *not* a deviant minority," Potts, Diggory, and Peel assert; "they are a representative sample of women in the childbearing years within the community to which they belong . . . Induced abortion is found in all social, economic, educational, ethnic, and religious groups. In fact, it is one of the few activities in which nearly any individual can become involved . . ."[11]

Simone de Beauvoir is franker still. "There are few subjects on which bourgeois society displays greater hypocrisy," she writes. "For an author to describe the joy and suffering of a woman in childbirth is quite all right; but if he depicts a case of abortion, he is accused of wallowing in filth and presenting humanity in a sordid light. Now, there are in France as many abortions per year as there are births. It is thus a phenomenon so widespread that it must in fact be regarded as one of the risks normally implied in woman's situation."[12]

Normally implied, perhaps, but not generally accepted. Abortion may be a commonplace, but it is also one of the most widely kept secrets in our society. This routine hazard of sexual life has inspired hardly any folklore and very little imaginative literature. Only a handful of novels recount the experience. Only rarely do women pass the lore of their abortions on to their daughters or friends; only rarely do they exchange anecdotes over luncheon tables or counsel over the back fence. Millions upon millions of women who have been through abortions (and the millions of men involved as well) have simply buried the experience once it was over, hidden it, expunged it from their public selves.

"I finally had to tell my father," Marion admits. "And I couldn't believe it. He told me—and he's a military officer, very straight—that one of my aunts and my own older sister had had them years before, and illegally too."

"After I hunted all around for a doctor," Anne says, "I later found out that my own aunt had used one of the fanciest doctors in town."

But these invisible women don't often serve any other woman as favorable role models or help her find an acceptable image of herself in these circumstances. Thus, Zimmerman believes, a major task of the abortion passage, apart from negotiating some concrete solution to the problem pregnancy, is discovering what this unexpected crisis means in the larger context of the woman's life, values, and social world.

A woman may react to the news of her pregnancy with panic or steely calm; she may approach her dilemma chaotically or resolutely. She may know instantly what she will do or wrestle for weeks with her conscience and her desires. But the pregnancy marches inexorably on, a fact with important practical consequences.

Under the 1973 Supreme Court decision, abortion before twelve weeks is available to adult women, and to many minors, essentially on demand. The procedure itself takes under a quarter of an hour, requires only a local anesthetic, carries very little medical risk, and often costs less than two hundred dollars complete. After the twelfth week the pregnancy enters the so-called second trimester and the abortion passes into a different legal and medical category. The further it progresses past this threshold, the more expensive, dangerous, and difficult the abortion becomes. After the twenty-fourth week, when the pregnancy passes into the third trimester and the fetus passes the threshold of viability, abortion is legally permissible only very rarely and is medically quite a major undertaking.

Although a woman thus has some leeway to decide, it is not as great as it appears. Doctors discuss pregnancy in *menstrual weeks*, or weeks since the first day of the last menstrual period (also written: weeks LMP). Conception most often occurs in the middle rather than at the beginning of the menstrual cycle, so a woman called ten weeks pregnant is generally carrying only an eight-week-old fetus. The clock began to run two full weeks before she ever conceived. Although this system makes little emotional sense, it does have a certain physiological logic; the date of conception often cannot be accurately known, but the date of the last period usually can. And the menstrual flow marks the beginning of the process that makes conception possible.

Thus, a vigilant woman who suspects the possibility of pregnancy and acts with reasonable speed can obtain a quick and reliable urine test at her doctor's office or clinic, or do a somewhat less reliable test with a drugstore kit about forty-two days after her last period, or about two weeks after the next period should have begun. This type of test measures a pregnancy hormone, human chorionic gonadotropin (HCG) excreted in the urine. A more sensitive urine test can give results within days of the missed period but is less often used because it requires a wait of an hour and a half. More sophisticated, expensive, and rarely used techniques can spot HCG in the blood a scant week after conception, a full week before the next period is even due.

So even a vigilant woman is unlikely to have a definite result until six of the first twelve weeks have passed. And any one of a number of things can delay it still further. If she has irregular periods; if she menstruates despite pregnancy, as some do; if she has only mild or no swelling, nausea, fatigue, or tenderness; if she doesn't know the symptoms of pregnancy; or if, as many do, she simply denies the possibility of pregnancy and ascribes her symptoms to a cold, tension, or menstrual irregularities, then a positive diagnosis will take weeks longer. Joanne, for example, got her first hint from her dentist, who observed characteristic changes in her gums. Toni didn't know until an auto accident put her in the hospital. Often a watchful mother has been the first to spot a teenager's expanding waistline several months after conception.

The most commonly used pregnancy tests may produce a good many false negatives (and some false positives). If the test is done too early, or with diluted urine, or if the woman has used certain drugs (including marijuana) or has certain glandular conditions, the results may be wrong. The strong urine from the first urination in the morning is most reliable.

Thus, a positive urine test constitutes a strong likelihood of pregnancy but not a definite diagnosis. If the period does not begin within two weeks of a negative result, a second test is advisable. Any woman who thinks she is pregnant should also have a pelvic examination to determine not only that pregnancy exists but that it is normal. The laboratory urine tests, for example, do not distinguish between a healthy pregnancy and a potentially life-threatening ectopic pregnancy; in the latter case the embryo implants not in the uterus but elsewhere, such as the fallopian tubes or even in the abdominal cavity. No ectopic pregnancy can be carried to term, and all must be surgically removed. Untreated, it can rupture the fallopian tube, damage other organs, and cause intense pain, hemorrhage, infection, even death. The combination of a positive urine test and a negative pelvic exam thus merits very careful scrutiny. A pelvic exam can also detect certain dangerous tumors.

A skilled physician also uses a pelvic exam to get a very accurate idea of the pregnancy's length. Recollections of when the last period began or conception could have occurred often prove hazy, but this information can be vital if abortion is contemplated. Thus, any woman who suspects she might consider abortion needs to be examined by a doctor familiar with the gradual changes of the early weeks, not just by any old physician. Dr. Samuel Barr, a pioneer in abortion services, notes that "until the recent advent of legal abortion, it was not worth training gynecologists how to tell the subtle differences in the size of the uterus between eight and nine weeks, ten or eleven weeks, or most important, between twelve and thirteen weeks."[13] For generations the great majority of doctors learned merely to tell the pregnant from the nonpregnant uterus because that was all a law-abiding physician needed to know. To be certain how far along she is, a woman thus needs a physician especially attuned to the requirements of abortion.

Many free-standing abortion clinics offer pregnancy tests and pelvic examinations at moderate cost and without obligation. So do Planned Parenthood clinics, community health centers, and many hospitals. Where one has the pregnancy test done in no way determines whether or where an abortion will follow. But it may importantly influence a woman's experience, whatever her decision.

"The role of a doctor who is intellectually honest is to acquaint a patient with the material facts of a problem and to recommend and review courses of action in light of potential benefits weighed against possible risks," Barr writes.[14] It is not to impose his own values on the woman's future, nor to mislead her about her true situation until it's too late to act, nor to comment on the wisdom or morality of her decision about her own future, nor to evaluate the appropriateness or inappropriateness of her sex life, nor to exaggerate the physical or psychological dangers of abortion. And yet some doctors do all these things, and also send women to "counseling" or "referral" services whose true purpose is dissuade anyone and everyone from abortion.

"He sort of leered and said, 'If you play with fire, you're going to get burned,'" Ellen says.

"He sent me to a counselor," Terry recalls, "and she

showed me gory pictures of fetuses and kept calling them 'babies.' She really pressured me not to abort."

Some doctors, of course, hold conscientious scruples against abortion in general or in a particular case. No physician of integrity will abrogate his or her own moral code for a patient's convenience, any more than he or she will use a position of trust and authority to impose a personal moral opinion on another. A physician of integrity will tell a patient, "It's your right to decide on abortion, but if you do I can't help you with it any further. These are the facts of your condition, and here is how to find someone who can."

Medical people hold a wide range of opinions on abortion. Dr. Curtis Boyd, a Texas gynecologist well known as a pioneer in second-trimester procedures, recalls the tense meeting at which his application to a New Mexico county medical society was heard. Local doctors knew he intended to establish the county's first abortion facility. Some spoke strongly against him, often on moral grounds, and others equally strongly argued for him. Admission of qualified candidates is usually pro forma and rarely inspires any floor debate at all.

Most clinics that specialize in abortion and related services, however, have a feminist orientation; many, indeed, grew out of the women's and consumer movements. Thus they view the act of abortion itself as morally neutral and the decision as within each woman's own discretion. They are prepared to support a woman's position, whatever it may be, so long as it represents an honest reaction to her situation. Such clinics will not present unsolicited moral opinions along with the results of a pregnancy test; for women who fear the reaction of their own doctors, or who have no doctor to consult, they offer medical information without moral strings.

Finding such a clinic or doctor presents little problem in large metropolitan centers, but in smaller places abortion facilities can be very sparse indeed. The great majority of U.S.

counties have no abortion facilities at all. Nonetheless, most women probably know, but may not realize that they know, someone who can recommend a good doctor or clinic, either by personal experience or reputation. Commercial referral or counseling services are less dependable; they may put their own desire for kickbacks or fees above an individual woman's best interests, and they may be intake points for pro-life agencies. A ready source of reliable information and sound referrals is the toll-free hotline maintained by the National Abortion Federation, a professional association of abortion providers whose member organizations must meet recognized ethical and medical standards. A call to 1–800–772–9100 (or 546–9060 from the Washington, D.C., area) will provide answers to questions and names of nearby facilities.

Obvious though it may seem, however, information and referrals can only help women willing and able to face the central fact of their situation: They are pregnant despite their desire not to be. But a substantial proportion of women do not acknowledge their problem in time to seek the simplest and safest remedy, and this delay means they may need a riskier and costlier second-trimester abortion. From a worldwide survey of abortion practices Henry David concludes that "in the United States, late abortions occur most frequently among economically, educationally, and socially disadvantaged women, and especially among very young teenagers."[15] David calls them women, but many of them think of themselves as girls—girls who have never been clearly told how conception happens, girls too young to know much about birth control, girls certainly too young to conceive of themselves as women capable of giving birth. But the steady drop in the age of menarche (onset of menstruation) over the past couple of generations means that millions of adolescents are at risk of becoming pregnant, and about a million, in fact, conceive in the United States each year.

An unwanted pregnancy is a difficult enough emotional and practical problem for a mature and sophisticated woman who possesses knowledge, money, experience, and contacts.

For a young girl confused about her options, isolated from the medical system, terrified of her parents' reaction, and lacking funds or the habit of independent action it can be an almost unbearable disaster. How much easier, then, to ignore the symptoms, to deny the possibility, to believe that "I'm too young to get pregnant," or "It can't happen if he pulls out," or "You can't get pregnant the first time." How much more comforting to ascribe the symptoms to some other cause, or deny that they even exist.

Abortion counselors see this type of denial often enough to consider it a major cause of late abortion. "By the time the pregnancy is so obvious that not even they can deny it," says one, "it's also too late for a simple first-trimester procedure." As we shall see in a later chapter, it also may figure importantly as a reason why some women have to go through the whole grim experience a second time.

2/

TAKING
IN THE NEWS

"They lay as if paralyzed by what they had done . . .
like a city struck out of a quiet sky by an atom bomb. All
lay razed; all principle; all future; all faith; all honorable
intent."

John Fowles

Scholars don't agree on the origin of the word "shock," but
some trace it back to an Old French root meaning "collide."
If they're right, it perfectly describes the situation of a
woman whose worst fear has just become a reality in a positive test for HCG: Her hopes, her plans, her self-esteem have
crashed head-on into the immovable fact that she's pregnant.
Whole chunks of her life and self-image have probably broken loose in the smashup, and she'll somehow have to put
them back together.

But now, at first, there's no time to think about long-
range repairs. Right now she's stunned and merely reacting,
or—if she has an extraordinarily cool head—thinking about
limiting damage and getting first aid. "It took me a little
while just to take in what the doctor told me," Bonnie says.
"Not what the words were, but what each one of them *meant*.
I couldn't even think about what the *situation* meant for some
time afterward."

"When I was a house mother," Helen recalls, looking

back almost twenty years on a similar scene of wreckage and confusion, "one of my freshman girls thought she was pregnant and came to me. In all innocence I suggested she find out for sure and then begin canvasing the possibilities. She assured me it would 'kill' her parents, and indeed it seemed reasonable to suppose that it would 'kill' mine, and I ended up getting much too involved and very close to facilitating an abortion for her—when her parents figured out what was going on. And not only did it *not* kill them, but they made arrangements with their family doctor, who, it turned out, had taken care of virtually every woman in the family."

To those two panicky young women, Helen marvels, this outcome seemed both a deliverance and a mystery. And it remained so to Helen for some time afterward. "This was the early sixties," she continues, "and not until my own daughter was born did I realize that obviously every parent has the possibility of this scenario in mind from the beginning. It was an extravaganza of naïveté." And of anxiety, shame, and secrecy. It was a moment when normal ways of handling life failed and something else took over.

"There are times in the life cycle of women," some experienced psychologists have observed, "when physical events become the focus around which other aspects of life are organized."[1] Even an intelligent, purposeful woman who had believed life to be under her control, or at least her volition, suddenly finds that—of all things—her body is in charge. Physical processes, not her plans or ambitions, draw the outlines of the future. The onset of menstruation is one such time, and menopause another, but for most women pregnancy is the most significant of all. "I knew that someday—in the distant future—I wanted to have kids," Bonnie says. "But I never really thought about what that would mean, or when, or how. I would just someday be in the right situation and it would happen. But for now I just expected to go along with my life, more or less as I wanted to, for simply years and years." And then suddenly, and probably without warning, anatomy is, if not destiny—to use Freud's term—then at least the immediate and pressing future. Time compresses, collapses, and the future becomes now.

Even for women who want, and have sought, to become pregnant, finding out for sure is a jolt. As many as 85 percent of the married women in one study—women socially and psychologically "set" for eventual motherhood—reported "marked disappointment and anxiety" when they learned of their first pregnancy.[2] A woman usually knows very little about pregnancy before her own time comes. And that little does not adequately prepare her for giving her body and her future over to something growing inside her—"a new life" for Margaret, "a kind of tumor that can destroy me" for Bonnie. "It was unknown and a little fearful," said a woman who even welcomed her pregnancy.[3]

But if Helen sees more clearly in retrospect, at the time she gave her advice to Susan, her young charge, it appeared sound. In fact, neither Helen nor Susan had had any clear idea of how to proceed and reacted completely on instinct. How, indeed, could most women know how to react? No personal experience prepares them for news they never expected to hear, and very little folklore or tradition tells them what to do next. Unlike most of life's other common calamities, unwanted pregnancy provides no cultural script to follow, no etiquette to use as scaffolding for action and feeling. Although a woman with an unplanned pregnancy may be hurting badly, she doesn't count as one of society's recognized sufferers, with a rightful claim to sympathy and an acknowledged role to play. Indeed, in many people's eyes (including, perhaps, her own) she's to blame for her own trouble, more sinning than sinned against. Unlike the newly bereaved, for example, she has no loved ones to notify and no funeral to arrange; unlike divorcing spouses, she has no lawyer to consult and no property arrangements to consider; unlike the gravely ill, she has no medical advisor and no status as a patient. Unless she moves in quite sophisticated social circles, she stands alone, outside any social convention she knows about, with her single, unwelcome, and very problematic fact, a fact that she furthermore feels she must keep from many of those she'd normally turn to in times of trouble. Thus, because society doesn't tell her what to do, she can only fall back on her own resources of character and stamina.

Our culture has paid extraordinarily little attention to the entire lived experience of unplanned pregnancy, but without doubt we know least of all about this early stretch of the journey. Researchers have probed into why women conceive without wanting to, how they decide what to do about it, and what they undergo as they carry out their decisions and in the months and years afterward. But the earliest moments of the crisis, before the terms of discussion have even taken shape, remain as dark and private as the thoughts that come, unbidden, of a sleepless 3 A.M.

This ignorance should not surprise, of course. The moment is relatively brief, and its jumble of meanings and emotions are hard to distill in terms that can go into a dissertation, a computer model, or even a clear sentence. Most studies of the psychology of pregnancy involve married women who carry to term; the early reactions thus become harbingers of later mothering. Women with problem pregnancies, furthermore, usually don't even make themselves known to those professionally interested in their plight until somewhat later. They don't ordinarily appear in counselors' offices or in social scientists' samples until they present themselves at an abortion clinic or counseling center—until, in other words, they have imposed some order on the situation and have reached, or are approaching, a definite decision.

Those who have already decided against abortion, or who have become so frozen in inaction that the pregnancy simply overtakes them, naturally don't show up in these places at all. So, by the time women do appear, counselors and researchers have bigger fish to fry: "What have you decided? And how did you decide? And how do you feel about it?"

In a certain sense, though, this brief early period may be the most crucial of all. If, as Zimmerman suggests, a woman's great task is to decide on the meaning of her pregnancy, then the first hours or days are when she starts. She now makes choices so basic, so large, and perhaps so little acknowledged as such that they cannot even be called decisions. They are what precedes decisions, the definition of the elementary terms on which decisions can be made.

This is also, for most women, the time of greatest stress. Ellen Freeman, who studied Philadelphia women undergoing abortion, found that they felt least comfortable, most anxious and depressed, after confirming the pregnancy but before doing anything about it.[4] Uncertainty is highest now, and the problem most problematic, because a woman may not have even sorted out the terms of her predicament. Much talk and writing suggest that women promptly and unmistakably feel one of two distinct, immediate, and recognizable responses to pregnancy: wanting or not wanting. But experience is usually more complex.

In puzzling over the apparently anomalous behavior of Catholic women, for example, sociologist Patricia Steinhoff makes an illuminating point about volition. Most studies, she observes, show that despite their church's unequivocal ban, Catholics represent a percentage of abortion patients at least equal to, and often larger than, their proportion in the general population. But since Catholics become pregnant more often than others, they may "still be choosing abortion less frequently . . . This suggests that Catholic women may be less likely to prevent pregnancy and *less likely to define it as unwanted when it occurs.*"[5] (emphasis added)

Less likely to define it as unwanted. Steinhoff sees wanting emerge not as a sudden, unitary reaction but as part of a larger, more complex approach to an entire situation. Wanting turns out to be, in the vulgarized psychological term, part of a woman's whole gestalt. And like the Gestalt theorists' famous picture that becomes, according to the viewer's choice, either a champagne glass or a pair of kissing profiles, the unplanned pregnancy can take on more than one shape. Leslie, for example, married, in her late thirties, and on the verge of a possible new career (but one that frightens her a bit), saw an unexpected pregnancy as both an obstacle and an opportunity. "I didn't know whether I really wanted to start looking for a job or whether I wanted to stay home with one more baby—one that would certainly be my last, and would be more delicious because of that. I really didn't. When the doctor told me, I didn't know whether to be happy or sad. I couldn't figure how I should present it to Tom—he'd be sure to say, 'Whatever you want is OK.' It was a strange sensation. I wanted both these things and neither of them. How I felt depended on what I thought about."

Sorting out, of course, doesn't necessarily happen consciously, any more than an unsuspecting viewer "decides" which to see first, the goblet or the lovers. Indeed, such very basic decisions occur outside of rationality, in that special area of knowledge and deduction known as intuition. And as this realm of knowledge lies outside the strict boundaries of reason, it can contain inconsistent, even contradictory, ideas and feelings. Many women pregnant for the first time, even those deeply fearful, anxious, or angry about the pregnancy, feel an intense relief, a kind of gratitude that they can, in fact, conceive. They rejoice in this confirmation of future possibilities, even as they work to keep them from coming true in the present. An emotional ambivalence may thus underlie the whole experience: wonder that it could happen at all; sorrow that it had to happen now.

Also playing a vital role is a woman's customary approach to crisis. Does she generally lead with her mind or her emotions? Does she stand on her own feet or lean on others? Does she already know what she wants or must she still find out? If she must find out, does she know how? To whom and how does she look for help? And, finally, what does she see as the problem?

Helen's young charge Susan, for example, defined the situation emotionally and, having few resources of her own, turned to an older, and presumably more experienced, young woman. To her the core of the problem was keeping knowledge from her parents. Leslie, on the other hand, reacted more rationally and looked into herself for a solution. For her the core of the problem was knowing her own mind. These two reactions, Zimmerman would suggest, represent more than individual differences between two women; here circumstances profoundly alter cases.

Zimmerman views a woman's situation in the broadest possible terms to include not only her social and economic circumstances but her stage of personal development. A woman both old and young enough to become pregnant, she believes, has reached one of four points on her road to adulthood. Until age eighteen or so she lives in "late childhood," economically and socially dependent, and still very much a daughter in her parents' household. She identifies herself primarily in terms of her family and has yet to begin prying her own identity free. For many young women the stage of "first independence" comes next, corresponding roughly to the college years. During this period of "searching" she tries on adult roles and identities without committing herself definitely to any. Her adult life remains uncertain, undefined, and in the future; she has yet to choose among her options.

These same years of eighteen to twenty-two, however, may see a woman "entering [her] adult vocation." Although possibly no older than someone in the previous stage, she has "made a choice about [her] adult life." She has taken some conscious steps to narrow her options; she has begun to define who she is and thus who she will be. She might, for example, have committed herself to an engagement or marriage, or perhaps to a demanding career choice that will exclude marriage for a while at least. And a somewhat older woman, "established in [her] adult vocation," has narrowed her choices down to a few, and these she has put into action. She does a specific kind of work, has established central relationships with specific persons, and knows the particular direction she wants her life to take.[6]

Narrowing her options to a concrete few better equips a woman to react concretely to a pregnancy. Finding herself pregnant, particularly for the first time, presents a woman with a basic identity decision: whether or not to become a mother now, and by this man.

"Almost all females want babies," writes psychologist Myra Leifer; "90% of all women in the United States aged 18 to 34 said that they expected to have or had had at least one child."[7] In talking with women pregnant for the first time, she found that "for all the women, even those for whom the pregnancy was unplanned, the central issue was not whether to have children, but when to begin a family. These women universally recognized children as a basic part of the meaning of life, as central to their view of themselves as women."[8] But the meaning of this particular pregnancy depended on whether they believed themselves ready to undertake motherhood. Women knew strongly, and intuitively, whether they possessed "an inner sense of readiness to have a child." Those with it faced their pregnancy with equanimity; those without it suffered "intense feelings of psychological unpreparedness . . . disbelief . . . anger . . . despair."[9]

Glenda, for example, had no "good" reason not to continue her pregnancy. Her husband, Chet, a graduate assistant, earned enough to support them both in their university town, and looked forward to an apparently bright future as a professor. A young wife in the mid-1960s, she could easily have followed most women in her position: accepted the accident as fate, ended or interrupted her own graduate work, postponed her own career hopes, and let the pregnancy run its course. Emily, in grad school at the same time, fitted not one but two unplanned pregnancies into the hectic years of her own and her husband's comprehensive exams and dissertation research. But Glenda "didn't feel ready." And by this she alludes not to some vague failure to prepare but to a deep, undeniable rebellion of her soul. So she and Chet took the hard way—an expensive, anxious, awkward illegal abortion. "I don't see what else I could have done," Glenda says. "I felt as if I were drowning."

And in a very real sense Glenda's "I" would have

drowned in motherhood. She would have lost her sense of identity as it was then, her notion of who she was and what she would be. Motherhood—and especially a first pregnancy —signals a basic threat to a woman's established self. "I knew that I would stop being just me," Maureen said, "and be Mother for ever and ever." Dreaming herself back into her own childhood, Maureen saw Mother not so much as a person with private wishes and predelictions but as the rock-solid ground of her emotional life. "I knew that I would have to be that, for someone else, for the rest of my life. My life as a person who could think only, or even mainly, of myself was over."

As psychologist Lucy Scott learned in talking with women in their late twenties and early thirties who have intentionally avoided motherhood, identity—who "I" am and will be—is the central issue. "I'll probably go on postponing the final decision," one of Scott's informants said.

> I think that having to come to terms with the decision is like coming to terms with the fact that you can't have it all in life. I feel that up to now in my life I've always been able to do what I wanted, and I've never been denied anything important. In this decision, I'm going to be denied something important one way or another— either my freedom or the experience of being a mother. So I do feel torn. I spend a lot of time thinking about what it really means to "have it all."[10]

Zimmerman doesn't specifically discuss the mature person, well past college age, who has not yet resolved the practical meaning of her fertility. But because, as Scott observes, "the decisions a woman makes about her reproductive function are a central developmental issue in her life,"[11] such women, who represented more than half of those Scott studied, "have developed and maintained a flexible and diffused female role identity by keeping all their options open and have, in a sense, postponed the task of identity formation.

They have placed a high priority on 'giving birth to themselves' . . ."[12] Their own meaning of womanhood does not
now—and perhaps never will—include the notion of being
"Mother for ever and ever." That of a woman who willingly
embraces her pregnancy must at some point begin to do so.

Zimmerman and Scott, with their different goals, asked
different questions of different people, yet it does not seem
unreasonable to apply the insights of one to the findings of
another. The women with the least-defined adult identities,
Zimmerman found, those least tied into a particular vision of
themselves as mature women, had the most difficulty taking
in the news of their pregnancies. They more often reacted
emotionally than rationally; they hunted more frantically for
meaning and help.[13]

An adult identity, of course, implies an attitude toward
sexuality, a vision of oneself as a sexual being, and an understanding of sex as integral to life. This is why, as Helen observed, "every parent has the possibility of this scenario in
mind," even if he or she does not communicate as much to a
young daughter. But the sexuality of the not-yet-adult
stretches as an open chasm between the generations. It even
became a political issue when the federal government attempted to impose a "squeal rule" requiring birth control
clinics to inform parents of prescriptions given to minors.
Knowing the dangers and temptations that sex harbors for
the unwary young just bringing their adult selves into being,
conscientious parents often try to keep their children safe by
keeping them from sex. But this strategy often results in setting a higher moral standard than many young people can
maintain—higher even than the parents themselves may have
maintained. The young man in the film *The Graduate*, for example, was astonished to learn that his girlfriend had been
conceived in the backseat of a Chevrolet—something he
thought only people of his own generation could do.

The children, still too innocent to realize their parents'
didactic intent, and still too literal-minded to know the difference between appearance and reality, take the parents at their

word. In many homes, therefore, what is in fact the fond hope that "nice girls don't" passes for a description of reality. "Kids who are sexually active don't want their parents to know, I guess, because they fear rejection or animosity," observes Cheryl, a thoughtful high school student. "It's a very emotional thing where they feel like they've failed their parents."[14]

This is the flip side of Susan's certainty that her news would "kill" her parents. What it killed was her image of herself as an entirely "good girl" and the convenient fiction of her innocence.

It also "killed" the social Susan as she was then. Pregnancy, after all, is not only a physical condition; it is also a social role. Being pregnant involves not only carrying a fetus but having other people know about it. At its best, even for the healthy young wife of a prosperous husband, pregnancy has its social contradictions. It means gaining prestige, as the embodiment of fertility, but also losing it, as an increasingly ungainly figure. And at its worst, for the woman who socially "can't" be pregnant, it means social disaster.

For the person with a "spoiled identity," the sociologist Erving Goffman observed, for the person who falls into some stigmatized category, the greatest challenge of social life is managing who knows what; a few insiders must be permitted to know the truth, which must be kept from all others to preserve social standing. And few identities are more "spoiled" than that of the woman "improperly" pregnant. For her, keeping the good opinion of those she values may take on overriding importance. Of eighty women pregnant outside of marriage who talked with British psychologist J. F. Pearson, for example, fewer than half told either parent. Of those who eventually decided to abort, only 20 percent confided in their mother or father. And almost 90 percent thought it unlikely that anyone beyond their few confidantes would ever find out. Indeed, Pearson believes, fear of disclosure may even have motivated many of these abortions. A woman who aborts early need never be "socially" pregnant.

"Women more sensitive to the possibility or experience of being discredited were more likely to have the pregnancy terminated," he concludes.[15]

Pearson's women ranged from seventeen to thirty years of age, but sociologist Rae Hudson Rosen found a similar pattern among teenagers, even when living at home and almost twenty years after Susan. Only half of the pregnant girls she spoke with confided in the mothers living under the same roof (and almost none before the pregnancy was confirmed). The other half continued their customary pattern of not speaking with parents about sexual matters and handled the situation on their own.

In general, Rosen found, parents and teenagers simply don't talk about sex, period. But rather than arising from mindless parental prudery, she believes, "such evasion . . . springs from mutual desires to avoid disruptions of family relationships and conflict over different standards of sexual conduct."[16] In striving to guard their daughters from danger, parents remember that their own youths held few nastier traps than unwanted premarital pregnancy. A man or woman could hardly have grown up in America before abortion became legal without seeing young lives stunted, distorted, or even ended by "getting into trouble." There were the anguished searches for abortionists; the dangerous, harebrained methods—falling down stairs, drinking toxic potions —to "get rid of it"; the hasty, ill-advised, and ultimately fragile marriages to avoid disgrace; the premature end of schooling and of youth; the mysterious "rest cures" at far-off sanatoria for vague diseases that lasted several months. There was even the occasional girl like Rita, whose father died of a heart attack shortly after she returned, pregnant and unmarried, from a Junior Year Abroad, and whose neighbors ever after whispered about what had "killed" him. Many adults can't totally shake off the atmosphere of peril and dread that surrounded sexual experimentation in their young days. Even if the legal and moral world of the young is very different now, for many parents the well-remembered melody lingers on.

Modern children may not understand the cause of their parents' apparently inexplicable medievalism, but they certainly sense its emotional overtones. And though, as Rosen concludes, modern parents may not disapprove nearly as much as their own parents did, children still do not often care to find out.

Susan's distress, therefore, was no less real for being at least partially founded on a misapprehension. It loomed large in the experience of her pregnancy right up to the point that a practical solution appeared. And for nearly every other woman in her situation distress is a constant, unavoidable companion. But the anxiety, fear, depression, and agitation generally don't become so severe as to constitute a serious concern in themselves. Even women who wish to be pregnant, after all, feel these emotions to some degree. Even the voluntarily pregnant often find themselves much more dependent on fate and on other people than they would like to be. And, as Freeman and others observed, distress nearly always drops sharply once a plan is put into action.

The practical question, therefore, is the degree of distress. Some women become so agitated or depressed that they simply can't deal with the decisions that lie before them; but the same thing also happens to some women who know from the start that they want their pregnancies to continue. In such cases talking with someone experienced in pregnancy counseling often helps. A staffer at a good abortion clinic, a clergy member, or a student personnel worker can generally help define and clarify the issues at stake in the pregnancy, as can some general counselors. It's important to remember that the woman probably needs only short-term crisis intervention, not full-scale therapy.

When should a woman seek more formal help in coping than her own friends or relatives can provide? As with much else in these difficult days, she probably must depend first on her own intuition. But, suggests psychologist Joan Offerman-Zuckerberg, who has worked with many troubled pregnant women, an extreme form of any of the normal reactions might mean trouble. She advises pregnant women to seek professional help if they experience the following:

> Excessive worries or fears . . . Unusual fantasies or thoughts experienced as 'out of control' . . . Acute or prolonged separation anxiety, serious depression, agitation, regression, etc. . . . Loss of emotional responsiveness . . . Unusual mood swings without source.[17]

Extreme lethargy, the refusal to formulate any plan to meet the emergency, is also a possible danger signal.

In the emotional turmoil of the first hours or days, most women find a thread of feeling, of meaning, that will lead them through the decisions of the coming weeks. They either want the pregnancy or they do not. It is either an opportunity, a gift, or a potential disaster. Only honest introspection can tell her which. Professional support may be a very good idea for some highly troubled women, but for many others it may prove unneccesary or even deleterious. Long after the emergency has passed, long after a woman has arrived at the life beyond this pregnancy, she will probably see that, however it came out, she won something from the experience. And that prize will probably be the knowledge that she could rally the strength, the discipline, and the ingenuity to meet it.

3/

THINKING
ABOUT
MORALITY

"It is obvious that the values of women differ very often
from the values which have been made by the other sex
. . . it is the masculine values that prevail."

—*Virginia Woolf*

In the spring of 1962 a respectable Arizona matron came to a
frightening realization. First, her husband, a physician, had
brought back from Europe some new sleeping pills not yet
available in the United States. Then she began to notice news
stories about French, German, and British children born
without arms and legs, with flippers where their shoulders
and thighs should have been; researchers eventually tracked
these horrifying deformities to a new German sedative taken
by their mothers during pregnancy. And the pregnant Sherri
Finkbine remembered that she, too, had taken thalidomide.

Mrs. Finkbine arranged to have her pregnancy quietly
terminated in a local hospital under its small quota of "therapeutic" abortions. But word got out, the hospital reneged,
and the fate of Sherri Finkbine's baby competed with the
sudden death of Marilyn Monroe for the nation's headlines
that summer. Finally, amid worldwide controversy, she trav-

eled to Sweden, where doctors aborted her severely deformed fetus, and at last she sank gratefully back into her previous relative obscurity—but not before becoming the first American woman in living memory so publicly to request and receive an abortion.

When, on January 22, 1973, the Supreme Court ruled in the case of *Roe* v. *Wade* to overturn Texas's and, incidentally, nearly the entire nation's existing abortion laws, four generations of Americans had grown up knowing that voluntary abortion was illegal in all but a very few cases, and believing, therefore, that it was nearly always wrong. The Finkbine case had raised some questions, and the 1963–65 German measles epidemic, by producing tens of thousands of deformed, deaf, blind, and retarded babies, had raised some more. A number of independent-minded doctors and clergymen had spoken out about the pathetic walking wounded who filled the gynecology wards, victims of butchery by ill-trained illegal abortionists. A handful of jurisdictions had liberalized their laws in the five years preceding the Court's decision, but even in those places the respectable medical establishment would have almost nothing to do with "nontherapeutic" abortion; every one of the states had prohibited it for at least eighty years.

For most of those years Americans "knew" what they thought of abortion: It was something done by shady people in desperate circumstances or, very rarely, a "therapeutic" medical procedure administered to women who could document their mental or physical unsoundness. For most of those years, in fact, few Americans not personally caught up in the drama of an unwanted pregnancy ever thought about abortion in any concrete way at all. For some it was a brief nightmare episode of cryptic phone calls; secret appointments at sleazy addresses; frantic, exorbitant payments; degradation; lying; pain; and fear. For most it was an infraction as bizarre as white slaving, as exotic as an opium den, as sordid as a house of ill repute; certainly nothing that nice people knew anything about.

And the great majority of Americans believed this to be the natural order of things, that abortion, in all but a very few cases, was just obviously and inherently wrong. Strangely enough, though, had Sherri Finkbine's great-grandmother wished an abortion for any frivolous or grave reason whatsoever, she would merely have had to look in the classified section of her newspaper, go to an address announced on a billboard, or write away for a product touted in a ladies' magazine. "To put the matter simply," writes James C. Mohr in his groundbreaking history of abortion law, "American public opinion tolerated the practice of abortion in 1850."[1] Respectable opinion, if not exactly countenancing it, certainly did not strongly object. Abortion was simply one of the many things that sophisticated people knew happened but ladies and gentlemen did not discuss. The great shift to seeing abortion almost wholly as a matter of right and wrong still lay in the future.

Some people, of course, had felt strongly against abortion during its years of legality before the Civil War, but they were not clergymen, politicians, or average citizens. They were doctors of medicine. Today we cast the debate about abortion almost exclusively in moral terms, in the language of ethical rights and duties, which taps into deep reservoirs of conviction among the public at large. But, as Mohr shows, the earlier campaigners against abortion, who achieved its almost universal prohibition, fought mainly along more practical lines and enunciated the professional interests and moral insights of a particular small elite.

Well into the middle of the nineteenth century most Americans saw nothing wrong with early abortion. As they then understood fetal development, the unborn child was inert until the "quickening" (literally, coming to life) signaled the start of its animate existence. Before the mother felt the first kicks, people believed, abortion could not kill anything because the fetus was not truly alive. Doctors of medicine trained in medical schools did not share this belief, however. Their more scientific knowledge of embryology taught them that the quickening marked no significant milestone in fetal development. They also took seriously the Hippocratic oath, which included the promise that "I will not give a woman an abortifacient." But theirs was distinctly a minority view. Before the days of widespread family planning, abortion served not so much as a form of fertility control but as the accepted, if regrettable, last resort of the unmarried girl seeking to avoid sure disgrace or the unfortunate married woman fearing a particularly severe childbirth.

No such thing as medical licensure existed in those days, and anyone who could attract customers could set up as a physician or curer. All kinds of people practiced abortion: experienced lay midwives, trained doctors, untrained but knowledgeable folk healers, animal surgeons, ambitious druggists, various types of self-styled scientists, and outright quacks. Methods included both surgical procedures of varying severity and all manner of potions, pills, capsules, douches, and infusions. Some methods worked, some didn't; some injured the woman, some were benign; some cost a lot, some were cheap. But in general the procedures of the successful abortionists were not conspicuously more dangerous than most other medical techniques of the day, nor, indeed, than childbirth itself. Abortion was "one of the first specialties in American medical history."[2]

By the middle of the nineteenth century all these methods and practitioners had multiplied rapidly. America had entered the stage of modernization that sociologists call the "demographic transition"; a nation with high birth and death rates had begun to change into one with falling birth and death rates. Americans, beginning with the well-to-do, now wanted to limit the size of their families. The abortionists' clientele no longer consisted only of terrified servant girls and desperate immigrants, but now included the native-born wives of prosperous men.

Thus, a number of interests flowed together in the doctors' crusade against abortion: desire to cut the intense competition for business by limiting medical practice to graduates of medical schools; concern to protect the public from dangerous charlatans; fear that a native old-stock birth rate lower than that of the immigrants would dilute the Anglo-Saxon character of the country; the ambition of M.D. graduates of medical schools to control medical practice in the United States; and, of course, the conviction that abortion was indeed homicide and thus morally wrong. "The fact that this belief coincided nicely with their professional self-interest is no reason to accuse physicians of hypocrisy," Mohr believes.[3]

By the years immediately preceding the Civil War, the American Medical Association, standard-bearer of the regular, school-trained physicians, had undertaken a nationwide struggle for control of medical practice, in which a ban on abortion was only a small side issue. In state after state they eventually won the day, convincing legislatures to outlaw medical practice by those without M.D. degrees and, incidentally, to prohibit abortion. And nearly always the banning of abortion was incidental to a much larger law regulating medical licensure and practice. By the early 1880s the prohibition was complete, and by the last decade of the century abortion once more was associated in the public mind with the poor and unwed. It apparently declined sharply among the respectable, in part because of advances in contraception, but also because of the legal risks it now entailed.

Thus, Mohr believes, abortion was outlawed in this country not because the ban expressed the moral beliefs of the people at large but because of a peculiar combination of historical forces. "To oversimplify greatly," he writes, "the two chief pressures that produced the antiabortion laws in the first place—the short-term interests of regular physicians in the face of an unprecedented crisis in the history of medical practice in the United States and the shift in the socio-demographic role of abortion in America—are truly unique historical circumstances."[4] The fact that later generations of Americans gave the ban an entirely different moral and social meaning in no way alters the circumstances of its original passage.

In a sense, understanding this historical background both simplifies and complicates the task of thinking about abortion today. On the one hand, we see that the period of prohibition represents not an unalterable American moral insight but rather the result of a particular coincidence of historical events. Unlike their twentieth-century descendants, most Americans of the Victorian period did not object to abortion per se on moral grounds (although they certainly objected to illicit sex and pregnancy). Indeed, not even the Catholic Church was then of one mind on the issue.

But, on the other hand, twentieth-century Americans must reject perhaps the main basis for abortion's general acceptability in Victorian times; scientific knowledge prevents us from sharing our ancestors' belief that the fetus is less alive after the quickening than before. We now know clearly that the fetus's physical life stretches without break back to the moment of conception and, indeed, even further back than that, into the individual lives of the egg and sperm that constitute it. We can no longer take refuge in the uninformed belief that early abortion puts an end to no living thing. Although we are once again legally free to act as the early Victorians did, we cannot accept the rationale they used to justify their actions. Rather, we bear the burden of deciding both the nature of that living thing and what that nature implies for moral action.

Indeed, the fact that we must "decide" rather than "discover" that nature is the core of the modern debate over abortion. No moral thinker on either side, be he a professor of theology or a teenager examining her conscience, disputes the idea that innocent human lives must be protected. But what the two sides cannot agree on, what stands at the center of the debate, is whether or when the fetus *is* a human life. We know that cells begin dividing almost as soon as the sperm meets the egg, but does this constitute, in any reasonable sense, a human life?

In terms relevant to the dispute, science gives no useful answer. The biologist Clifford Grobstein points out that fertilization initiates a new generation, not new life. The joining of a human egg and a human sperm produces a collection of cells that may or may not (but probably will, if left alone) grow into an undeniably human baby. But this same process occurs in all other animal species as well, and few dispute the morality of killing animals, for good reason, at *any* stage in their development. Human beings, at least in our culture, have a different moral standing from other animals; they enjoy certain rights and safeguards based solely on their humanity. But science can't tell us when they begin to enjoy those rights because science can only answer questions about physical nature, not those in the realm of values.

And the realm of values, not of science, is where this question lies. The Supreme Court said as much when, in *Roe v. Wade*, it refused to attempt any decision about when a mass of cells becomes a human person. Indeed, the Court's entire reasoning rests on its belief that if "those trained in the respective disciplines of medicine, philosophy, and theology are unable to arrive at any consensus," then in a secular democracy the decision rests with the individual conscience.[5]

For many years two basic positions have contended. One holds that from the moment of fertilization the fetus possesses sufficient attributes of humanity to make it a protected life, and that abortion is therefore homicide. Some people on this side of the argument would allow certain limited kinds of "justifiable homicide," but most probably would not.

The other position holds that the fetus, for at least part of its intrauterine existence, does not possess sufficient human attributes to make it a protected life, and that abortion is therefore not homicide. Many people on this side of the issue feel that late in pregnancy the fetus is enough like a baby to merit certain protections and, indeed, the Supreme Court permitted the states to forbid abortion in the third trimester unless the mother's life or health was at stake; but since the vast majority of abortions occur in the first twelve weeks, this limitation prevents very few women from obtaining abortions.

Put another way, the debate comes down to this:

Position A: The fetus is a human person and thus has the same right to life as any other human person.

Position B: The fetus—for at least part of the nine months—is not a human person and thus has no right to life that weighs against the mother's right to control the uses made of her own body.

Probably because they had the law on their side for ninety years, the antiabortionists generally have seized the oratorical high ground. They style themselves "pro-life," implying that those opposing them also oppose life. They claim to defend the family against attacks by its enemies. They have rallied awesome forces of respectability behind them: the fundamentalist wings of Protestantism and Judaism, the hierarchy of the Roman Catholic Church, and many conservative politicians. Theirs is a position that people loudly and righteously proclaim.

Many supporters of the pro-choice position, however, keep their opinions more private. The most coherent arguments in favor of the right to abortion come out of the feminist movement and use a feminist rhetoric unfamiliar and even threatening to many Americans. Favoring "choice," furthermore, hardly seems as elevated a cause as defending "life." The claim of women's freedom to determine their own destinies seems to many more traditional people nothing but the defense of frivolity and selfishness. Those who know from experience that this claim really means freedom from the terror of back-alley abortions largely keep their hard-won knowledge to themselves. Pro-choice backers come largely from the liberal segments of society: academia, the political left, the less traditional Protestant and Jewish denominations, the nonbelievers and the unchurched.

Because of their strategic advantage in the argument, the

antiabortionists have rarely had to defend their position on intellectual grounds. Historically the debate has consisted of the antiabortionists stating their positions and the proabortionists attempting to refute them. Rarely have the antiabortionists felt compelled to examine their basic premises. Years of close examination by opposing theologians, philosophers, and historians, however, have revealed sizable cracks in the foundation of antiabortion reasoning. Whether these cracks fatally weaken the entire structure is another question that only individual consciences can decide.

In this country the argument against abortion is Christian in its basis, founded on a particular interpretation of Christian notions about the nature of the human person. It also includes, according to Protestant theologian Beverly Wildung Harrison, the deep bias against women inherent in traditional Christianity. In its most extreme form this argument assumes that from the moment of conception (or some point very shortly thereafter) the fetus possesses the theologically most essential feature of a human being, namely, an immortal soul capable of salvation, and thus is a full human person apart from its mother. The fate of this soul, though not often mentioned in public debate today, figured in the thinking of earlier divines and perhaps in the debate's emotional intensity as well. St. Fulgentius wrote in the sixth century, for example, "It is believed beyond doubt that not only men who come to the use of reason, but infants, whether they die in their mother's womb, or after they are born, without baptism . . . are punished in eternal fire, because although they have no actual sin of their own, yet they carry along with them the condemnation of original sin from their very conception and birth."[6] Although not universally held, this view had a significant following.

Possession of a soul makes the fetus a person with a right to temporal life and a chance at salvation equal to that of all other human persons, including the woman carrying it in her body. As the rights of one human person cannot override the rights of another, the life of the fetus cannot be interrupted for the convenience or good of anyone else. In this argument's most extreme form, as stated by the Catholic Church, the fetus's life cannot be interrupted even to save that of the mother.

No woman, under this moral theory, ever has any right to stop a pregnancy; not Sherri Finkbine, anguishing over the probability of a thalidomide baby; nor Angela, whose severe diabetes might become much worse during pregnancy; nor fifteen-year-old Yvonne, carrying the product of a gang rape that happened on the way home from school; nor sixteen-year-old Kim, whose unintended pregnancy means being thrown out of her devout and punitive parents' home; nor Sarah, whose baby is doomed to die painfully before the age of four from Tay-Sachs disease; and certainly not Teresa, the abandoned mother of two normal sons, who stopped work and went on welfare in order to care at home for a baby daughter afflicted with spina bifida. Raymond, her heroin-addict husband, impregnated her by force on a rare, ugly visit home. Neither Teresa's terror that his drug habit means more birth defects; nor the exhausting, meticulous, round-the-clock care she must give her daughter; nor her virtual lack of material resources will, in the strict antiabortionist view, free her of the responsibility to carry her fourth pregnancy to term.

Jewish law, on the other hand, has never considered the child fully equal to its mother until its head appeared in the birth canal. Until that time the fetus is a part of its mother's body. The question of ensoulment (the entry of the soul into the body) or the soul's salvation does not enter Jewish thinking. "The conclusion is inescapable," writes Rabbi David M. Feldman,

> that these theological . . . reflections—or the actual spiritual destiny of the foetus—have no bearing on the abortion question . . . With the soul's immortality as much irrelevant as the time of its endowment, the earthly court must concern itself with the human problem of murder and deprivation of life in this world. For

the earthly court, law is defined: before birth, the embryo is not a person; from the moment of birth on, it is; the disposition of the soul, being pure to begin with, is unaffected.[7]

This does not necessarily imply, however, that the mother may frivolously dispose of that part of her body, any more than she can willfully injure any other part of her body, it being everybody's duty to preserve his or her health. Indeed, should the pregnancy threaten the mother's life or health, the doctor is not only permitted but required to sacrifice it to save her. Every living thing, the rabbis argued, has the inherent right to save itself from a "pursuer," whether innocent or not, that would destroy it.

The mother's life or health is arguably at stake, however, in very, very few pregnancies. The vast majority of abortion decisions concern less drastic considerations. And on these the rabbis are split. More permissive interpretations permit abortion to preserve her mental health (variously defined) and even to save her from anguish, including that of bearing a severely deformed child, or even, in some cases, from disgrace. No rabbi would, for example, justify an abortion like Sherri Finkbine's on the basis of the abnormality of a child; the handicapped have as much right to dignity and respect as anyone else. But the mental suffering of a mother who would have to see a child bear so hideous an affliction because of her own act would certainly, in the eyes of many rabbis, justify an abortion. "The foetus is unknown, future, potential, part of the 'secrets of God'; the mother is known, present, alive, and asking for compassion."[8] Different rabbis draw the line in different places, the more restrictive rabbis interpreting the boundaries much more narrowly and forbidding abortion in all but the gravest cases. In general, Feldman writes, "no woman is 'required to build the world by destroying herself.' This, of course, does not mean that ordinary pain, and certainly not social inconvenience, would come under this manifesto . . . Abortion, then, for ephemeral pain or for capricious reasons is clearly not intended here; in such cases, the 'warrants' and extralegal reverence for life play their part."[9] But still, the mother's concrete situation, her own suffering and distress, weigh heavily in the balance.

Jewish law, however, though intensely important to its adherents, is merely a sidelight on the national debate. Judaism has had no central authority for nearly two thousand years, and it commands the loyalty of only a small minority in the United States. The major battle, both theological and philosophical, has been argued on Christian grounds, and indeed, on the terms of the antiabortionists, primarily the Catholic Church.

Critics have concentrated their attacks on two crucial supports of the antiabortionist edifice of thought: the fetus's full personhood and its consequent rights. A rather abstruse debate among theologians concerns when the soul enters the body. Authorities as early and influential as St. Augustine have stated that "there cannot yet be said to be a soul in a body that lacks sensation when it is not formed in flesh and so is not endowed with sense."[10] We don't know exactly what St. Augustine meant by that opaque description, but clearly he believed that a human soul can only inhabit a human body, one, that is, with the features and structures of a recognizable human being. In his view the fetus doesn't qualify for at least the first few weeks, indeed, perhaps not until quickening.[11]

A number of more recent Catholic theologians, including St. Thomas Aquinas, have defended similar ideas. Some, such as the modern Jesuit Fr. Joseph Donceel, even assert that a belief in full ensoulment at the moment of conception threatens basic Church doctrine about the nature of Christ, both fully man and fully God, whose "saving power relates directly to the unity, in man or woman, of body *and* soul."[12] This unity requires that a human soul cannot exist in less than a fully human body; a tiny mass of undifferentiated cells doesn't meet his criterion. Theories that the soul enters the body at conception, according to this view, "contradict this nondualistic concept and advance an unacceptable dualistic view of human beings. This . . . conception . . . of human beings supposes that body and soul are two separate elements. Such thinking is profoundly anti-Christian"[13] and, indeed, was condemned as heresy by the Synod of Vienne in 1312.

But, argued Jean Gury, S.J., in 1864, "the fetus, though not ensouled, is directed to the forming of man. Therefore, its ejection is anticipated homicide."[14] This answer to the ensoulment argument has been called the "just in case" school of thought. Whether or not anticipated homicide amounts to the same thing as actual homicide, this is the official teaching of the Catholic Church, based on a series of Papal pronouncements beginning in the mid-nineteenth century. Paradoxically, however, despite the proclamation that a fetus possesses the same qualities of humanity as other persons, the Church does not act on this notion. No stillborn infant receives Christian burial; no impending miscarriage merits last rites.

Exactly when a fetus may or may not acquire a soul mainly interests doctors of divinity. What rights a fetus justly possesses concerns everyone trying to think about abortion. The classic right-to-life argument maintains that as a human person (regardless of how it got that way) a fetus, like all other human persons, enjoys an absolute right not to be killed. But from examining what this right means in practice, critics have concluded that the fetus cannot be called a full human person after all.

"When antiabortionists emphasize the obligation not to kill a fetus," writes philosopher Martha Brandt Bolton, "they make it seem as if our obligations to fetuses were as simple as our obligations not to kill other persons. This is seriously misleading. Fetuses differ from persons in that a woman cannot avoid killing a fetus unless she undertakes to nurture and develop it."[15]

"Not killing" another person requires only the discipline to refrain from deadly violence. "Not killing" a fetus, Bolton argues, requires at least a woman's commitment to place her body at the fetus's disposal for nine months. Unless the woman then arranges for adoption, it requires a good deal more.

Different people draw different conclusions from this fact. Dr. Bernard Nathanson, tortured by the memory of the thousands of abortions he has performed, yet equally tortured by the memory of the women he saw suffer and die after botched abortions, hopes for the day when science will make it possible to remove the fetus from an unwilling woman's womb and nurture it either in a surrogate's or on an artificial placenta. For him this foreseeable technology will resolve a painful moral dilemma. Until that time, though, he leans toward very strict limits on abortion.

Bolton and others, however, concentrate on overwhelming obligations in the here and now. Probably the best-known version of this argument is Judith Jarvis Thompson's famous essay about "unplugging the violinist." Suppose there were a famous violinist, she suggests, who had a rare and fatal disease. And suppose the only way the violinist could survive was to plug into a healthy person's body and use her organs as a life-support system. And suppose, finally, that serving as a life support meant that the healthy person had to considerably curtail her activities for an extended period of time. Is the healthy person required not to "unplug the violinist"? Must she continue to provide life support?

Certainly not, Thompson reasons. The obligation not to kill does not imply the obligation to offer one's own body as a heart, lung, and dialysis machine to an intrusive stranger. For Thompson an unwanted pregnancy is no more an invited guest than the grasping violinist. Although the Good Samaritan provides us an exemplary model of selfless behavior, he certainly far exceeds minimum requirements. All a person is required to do in good conscience, as one writer puts it, is to be a "reasonably decent Samaritan."

Indeed, in other areas of medical law the courts have not discerned any requirement for one person to save the life of another. William Head, a Louisiana leukemia victim, sued the University of Iowa Hospital to force it to divulge the name of a woman who had the right bone-marrow type to provide Head with a life-saving transplant. The hospital, maintaining the woman's right to privacy, won its case, as did a Pittsburgh man who refused to provide marrow for a dying relative who had sued to force him to become a donor.

By requiring a woman to go far beyond not killing, Bolton believes, the antiabortionist argument denies a woman the right to be "a responsible participant in a full moral life. The important fact about a pregnant woman's situation is the one I have emphasized: If she does not have an abortion, she must shoulder the more or less extensive and demanding responsibility of caring for the fetus."[16]

Thus, knowing the extent of her responsibility if she carries to term, the woman also has some idea of the extent of the resources of time, money, and care that she will need to fulfill that responsibility. And if she knows that she lacks them or can't assemble them, then carrying to term may, in Bolton's view, be an irresponsible choice. "No coherent moral rule requires a person to accept an obligation which she *knows* she cannot meet. Yet this is precisely what the antiabortionists' moral stance requires of a pregnant woman in this situation."[17]

Bolton's analysis makes clear that the strict antiabortion position doesn't give the fetus the same rights as full persons, but *more* rights. "Anti-abortionists insist on the fetus's right not to be killed; they discount the fact that a fetus has that right *only if* it also has a right to be nurtured by the pregnant woman and raised by her or someone else."[18]

Thus, the fetus of Yvonne, the rape victim, has a right to life only if it has the right to impose on her a constant, hateful reminder of her attack, and also to impose the obligation to love and care for a child whose very existence she loathes. Diabetic Angela's fetus has a right to life only if it has the right to destroy its mother's health. Teresa's has a right to life only if it has a right to deprive her gravely handicapped daughter of needed care. Do these rights come under the ordinary purview of "not killing"? Bolton thinks not.

In the strict antiabortionist view, Bolton believes, a woman's obligations to any fetus, even one implanted by a rapist, must override all the woman's other obligations, even those to retain her own sanity, safeguard her fragile health, or care for living dependent children. "Thus, throughout child-bearing years, a woman can act responsibly only by trun-cating her participation in activities in which others come to depend on her. But I think this is untenable, for it is central to the life of a morally responsible person to aspire to projects of this sort."[19] Thus, for Bolton the antiabortionist position on the rights of the fetus is flawed; it is not so much that the woman's rights outweigh those of the fetus but that those of the fetus do not legitimately outweigh those of the woman. In Bolton's view a "reasonably decent Samaritan" need not sac-rifice her own life, liberty, or happiness in order not to kill another.

Bolton's analysis, though, like much philosophical rea-soning, aims mainly to clarify what we mean by certain terms, such as "right to life." It does not necessarily aim to clarify how we should act in particular situations, and it cer-tainly doesn't aim to clarify how we might feel about them. It gives no good answer, for example, to Rachel, who agrees intellectually with Bolton's view but still says of the fetus she aborted, "You can't just say it's nothing. It's not a person equal to me, but I still know that I decided to end some kind of a life." When her relationship with the father dis-integrated, she saw no practical possibility of carrying her pregnancy to term without completely disrupting her life and alienating her family. Her own beliefs allowed her the right to end the pregnancy. Her mind can't find anything wrong with her decision, but she still looks back on a period of turmoil and sadness. "I had the sense that everyone de-serted me," she recalls, leaving her to make her decision alone. Part of her aloneness was the need to make an irrevoca-ble decision entirely on her own.

It's not fair to criticize Bolton's theory for not suc-ceeding at something it never set out to do, namely, answering doubts like Rachel's. But for Rachel any formulation based on what the philosopher Daniel Callahan has called "a strict calculus of rights and duties" is not enough. It simply does not describe the conflict she felt in coming to her decision. She needs an analysis that takes account of something more.

But, writes the Protestant theologian James M. Gustafson, "Every moral argument, no matter who makes it and what is the issue at hand, must limit the factors that are brought into consideration . . . In the ethics of abortion, the differences of opinion surface not only on the substantial moral question of whether it is permissible, but also on the question of what is the proper method of moral reflection."[20] No opinion takes everything into account. But what should be counted? Should we, for example, consider only the nature and rights of the fetus, as the strict antiabortion argument does? Should we admit religiously based concepts such as the soul, or should we concentrate on comparing the fetus's and the mother's rights, as Bolton does? Should we limit the fetus to only those rights that walking, breathing people have, or should we permit it some extra leeway because it is powerless to defend itself? There is no objectively right or wrong answer to these questions, but the answers one gives will determine the outcome of any train of moral reasoning. And for Rachel we must give more consideration to the nature of the fetus. She believes, like the philosopher Roger Wertheimer, that "it is not true that the fetus is a human being, but it is not false either."[21]

But many people like Rachel impose a further limitation on their reasoning: They refuse to take into account a religious concept such as the immortal soul. They need a theory of the fetus that accounts for their feelings without resort to the supernatural.

Probably the clearest such theory, and indeed one of the clearest of all considerations of abortion, is found in philosopher L. W. Sumner's brilliant book *Abortion and Moral Theory*. In it Sumner attempts to give a full account of the fetus, its rights, and the mother's responsibility to it, based entirely on secular principles. For Sumner neither the antiabortionist belief that the fetus has from the moment of conception an inalienable right to life at least equal to the mother's nor the pro-choice credo that the woman has complete control over her own body at all times, matches most people's intuitive understanding of the rights and wrongs of abortion.

He finds unjustifiable the demand that Angela carry her pregnancy to term at the sacrifice of her own health, or that Yvonne deliver a rapist's baby at the risk of her own sanity. But he also dismisses Linda's decision to abort because her boyfriend abandoned her midway through the pregnancy.

Sumner wishes to find out both the nature of the act of abortion and the relationship of the parties to it. In philosopher's language, he wants to know whether it is a private act or a moral one. A private act is one that affects no one but the actor; it is, quite literally, no one else's business. A moral act, on the other hand, is one that concerns someone other than the actor; it is thus always subject to moral considerations.

Now, in the strict antiabortion position abortion is always a moral act; the fetus is always a separate person fully equal to the mother. In addition, for those who think along religious lines, God is a party to every action; God's moral law rules all of life, and there can be, strictly speaking, no purely private behavior. Thus, for those accepting these two premises the physical act of abortion, for whatever reason, is always inherently wrong. In the strict pro-choice position, on the other hand, abortion is never a moral decision because the fetus is never a full party. Nor does God, or any other external arbiter, usually come into the picture. Thus, the act of abortion in and of itself is neither right nor wrong.

Sumner finds both of these positions equally untenable. Except by resorting to theology, he finds no way to distinguish the morality of early abortion from that of contraception; for him a newly combined egg and sperm no more constitute a "person" than either did separately. But he also finds no way to distinguish late abortion from infanticide; science tells us the birth represents no sharp break in the development of the fetus. But the broad consensus of our society (including the great majority of Roman Catholics) both rejects infanticide and accepts contraception, including devices like the intrauterine device (IUD) and the experimental morning-after pill, which presumably function after the egg has been fertilized. Most people, therefore, believe, in a rough-and-ready way, that a mass of undifferentiated cells is not the same thing as a nearly full-term baby waiting to be born.

So Sumner decides to incorporate into his philosophical theory the average person's insight that somewhere during a pregnancy the moral nature of the fetus changes. Somewhere it acquires the right to be considered as "another person" separate from the mother.

But when does this change take place? What features does the fetus acquire to be transformed from one type of being into another? Sumner rejects mere physical life as too broad and undefinable; if we accept the criterion that cells are alive in a moral sense, then an appendectomy, which removes living cells, must be considered killing. He rejects as too narrow the requirement that a "separate person" must possess a rational mind; people only develop rationality years after birth, so such a criterion could not protect newborns. He finally settles on sentience, the ability to experience sensation (e.g., pain) through the senses. The best medical opinion places its onset sometime late in the second trimester, and Sumner does not try to be more exact than that. "When we are dealing with the morality of abortion," he writes, "borderline fuzziness is both inevitable and tolerable. Many moral problems turn on factors that are matters of degree . . . It is a defect in a moral theory to draw sharp lines where there are none, or to treat hard cases as though they were easy."[22] Before this vague threshold of sentience, he believes, the fetus lacks moral standing and thus has no rights that weigh against the mother's; after passing this threshold it possesses moral standing, and its rights must be considered in the equation of rights and wrongs.

Thus, he concludes, "The moral issues raised by early abortion are precisely those raised by contraception."[23] If a fetus still lacking sentience has no right to be considered a separate person, then a woman who aborts it "violates no one's rights."

But, on the other hand, "the moral issues raised by late abortion are similar to those raised by infanticide." A sentient fetus with a right to life must be considered another person; aborting it definitely violates someone's rights. But Sumner still recognizes a "morally significant difference between abortion and infanticide," the fact that a fetus cannot live except in a mother's body. "That parasitic relation will justify late abortion more liberally than infanticide . . ."[24]

When the abortion occurs thus holds crucial moral meaning for Sumner. Seeing early abortion as an extension of contraception, he will allow it in cases like Rachel's, where contraception failed. The weeks before the fetus becomes sentient provide her with the moral room to act. But Sumner believes that if a woman knows of the pregnancy and does not act by the time the boundary to sentience has passed, then by her very inaction she has agreed to let the fetus acquire moral standing as a separate person. Barring some truly extraordinary circumstance, she has thus agreed to carry the pregnancy to term.

Take, for example, the case of Betsy, who ended a pregnancy that would have conflicted with a long-planned trip around the world. Some may find this reason frivolous, the very definition of abortion for convenience. But Sumner believes that if she acts early, say, as soon as she discovers the pregnancy, Betsy is well within her rights. The later the abortion, however, the graver Sumner believes the justification must be. This view, he thinks, expresses a basic American consensus. "One of the sentiments voiced by many people who contemplate the problem of abortion is that early abortions are importantly different from late abortions."[25] Among those people, of course, are the Supreme Court.

Sumner's may well be the most skillful restating to date of the moderate pro-choice position adopted by the Court. But despite his imaginative way of integrating many elements and objections into his closely reasoned theory, he still fails to reconcile the two basic positions. Indeed, he believes they cannot be reconciled by any theory at all. "These opposed views," he observes, "are imbedded within equally opposed ideologies concerning the status of women, the significance of marriage and the nuclear family, and the morality of sex and reproduction. On these larger issues, the principal parties to the abortion debate simply inhabit two different worlds."[26]

And, indeed, this is no mere figure of speech. At one time Americans may have more or less agreed on how the sexes should act: Women wore hats and gloves, not combat boots; men changed tires but never diapers. But when sociologist Ira Reiss asked Americans about sex, he found two basic sexual ideologies, two opposing images of the meaning of male and female. Although some people, like Rachel, find themselves unexpectedly and awkwardly caught between them— her mind in one place, her heart in the other—the distance between the two outlooks is large indeed.

The outlook Reiss calls "traditional-romantic" has dominated American life for generations. Many adults know it from old movies, from church, from the example of their parents. Suffused with guilt and bravado, this code marks a sharp difference between men and women, and between "good girls" and "bad girls." It enshrines the double standard, permitting adventure for men but only purity for women; it sees heterosexual coitus as the only possible goal of lovemaking, marriage as the only goal of love; and, most crucially, it believes that only "love redeems sexuality of its guilt, particularly for females."[27] A crucial point: Only love makes sex really OK, certainly not mere pleasure. And because they don't respond to brute sensation, nice girls didn't respond sexually, unless they loved the guy in question.

The outlook Reiss calls "modern-naturalistic" is a relative newcomer to our moral neighborhood. It sees sexuality as a physical function, not a moral anomaly. Stripped of its overlay of guilt, sex becomes a vehicle for mutual pleasure and, perhaps, intimacy. "Body-centered sex"—sex for physical pleasure alone—becomes acceptable for both men and women, although perhaps less valuable than "person-centered" sex, which concentrates on the relationship. But men and, most importantly, women may control the uses to which their own sexuality and bodies are put.

This is a crucial distinction because in reality the chasm between these two ideologies is the same one that divides the two sides of the abortion debate. Psychologist A. R. Allegeier and colleagues asked college students how they felt about abortion and what they thought about sex. Perhaps surprisingly, they found that the degree of guilt a person felt about sex in general quite accurately predicted his or her attitude toward abortion. The guiltier the person, the lower the approval of abortion. "Sex guilt," they conclude, is not an isolated attitude but a "generalized expectancy for sex-mediated punishment for violating or anticipated violation of internalized standards of moral behavior."[28] It has a strong emotional element and arises from clues picked up very early in life. "The formation of attitudes toward abortion may be at least partially due to the manner in which children and adolescents are taught about sexuality in general."[29]

The controversy thus concerns not only the rights of the fetus, the mother, society, or even God, but the very nature and purpose of sexuality, and thus the very nature and purpose of men and women, perhaps even of life on earth.

The Supreme Court brought this controversy to the surface when it established a woman's right to privacy as sufficient grounds for leaving the decision to her alone. Before *Roe v. Wade*, justifications of abortion, such as they were—and they were very little thought out and less discussed in public

—largely had to do with desperate attempts to save a woman from some more dreadful fate: public disgrace, financial ruin, mental illness, or death in childbirth. Indeed, abortion was part of the punishment for illicit sex.

"In those days," Jane recalls, "you took your life in your hands if you had an affair with someone you wouldn't marry or who couldn't marry you." But she and many of her career-girl friends did anyway, in the heady New York publishing world in the 1950s. And she and many of her friends paid the price in danger and fear; in Jane's case with a visit to an apparently legitimate doctor with a small—and very lucrative —side practice in D&C operations performed without an anesthetic. The doctor intoned moral precepts as he imparted the results of the rabbit test. But the idea that a woman could choose to put her body or her life to some other use than childbearing never entered the discussion. Indeed, unmarried girls aborted to make themselves once again "fit" for a "decent man" to marry.

These ideas are, in Sumner's word, "imbedded" very deeply inside the antiabortion argument. Harrison goes further, seeing them as implicit in our entire moral tradition. Despite its present preoccupation with the life of the fetus, the Catholic Church long viewed abortion as a primarily sexual sin and treated it as such in the early penitential literature. In the *Irish Canons* of the seventh century, for example, abortion ranks in seriousness about equally with illicit intercourse but well below homicide. The *Penitential Ascribed by Albers to Bede* of the eighth century notes:

> A mother who kils her child before the fortieth day shall do penance for one year. If it is after the child has become alive [she shall do penance] as a murderess. But it makes a great difference whether a poor woman does it on account of the difficulty of supporting [the child] or a harlot for the sake of concealing her wickedness.[30]

"Concealing her wickedness," of course, was then and has ever been a prime motive for abortion—and a prime reason for the Church's disapproval. A desire to suppress prostitution in Rome was, in fact, a basic motive behind the 1588 papal bull *Effraenatum*, in which Sixtus V outlawed all abortion on pain of excommunication. Bureaucratic complications, however, prevented this edict from taking full effect, and three years later Pope Gregory XIV rescinded it, advising that "where no homicide or animated fetus is involved, not to punish more strictly than the sacred canons or civil legislation does."[31]

But "wickedness" goes far beyond—or, rather, nowhere near as far as—prostitution. "The Church has consistently opposed abortion," writes historian of religion Jane Hurst,

> not only because of a suspicion that it is homicide, over which there is continuing debate, but because it is evidence of sexual sin. The church teaches that any act which intends to separate sexual union from procreation is sinful. A recent papal encyclical written by Paul VI states, 'Every marriage act must remain open to the transmission of life.' Abortion voluntarily obtained indicates that the sexual partners did not enter into their union with the intent to procreate. For this reason, abortion is always considered wrong.[32]

As Sumner observed, early abortion is morally inseparable from contraception.

A chasm yawns between the two sides on another question as well: Which considerations are they willing to take into account? As Gustafson observed, the classic antiabortion argument rests on particular assumptions about the nature of moral rules and moral reasoning. In a word, it rests on the concept of natural law, or moral truths inherent in the nature of the universe and obvious to all reasonable people. And it concerns itself almost exclusively with the physical act and with "the physician and the patient at the time of a particular pregnancy, isolating these two from the multiple relationships and responsibilities each has to and for others over long periods of time."[33]

Relationships and responsibilities, however, are what some observers believe most central to decisions to abort or not. Daniel Callahan, a practicing Catholic, writes the following in his anguished, exhaustive, authoritative critique of his church's position:

> Neither desperate poverty, mental illness, crippling physical disease, incapacity for motherhood, nor violent impregnation are allowed a place in the Catholic schematization of the problem. Any position which leads to so many exclusions, to so narrow a focus, merits rejection. The good it would accomplish is at the expense of other goods; the price exacted for the preservation of fetal life is too high a price.[34]

A well-trained philosopher, Callahan knows that he is attacking antiabortionist logic by a time-honored logical technique, *reductio ad absurdum*, or reduction to the absurd. If an argument, though faultlessly reasoned, arrives at an absurd conclusion, then one or more of its premises must be false. For Callahan the logical breaking point comes in the rare but instructive case when the mother's life must be sacrificed rather than kill the fetus. Catholic law presently permits no direct interference with the fetus to save the mother, only "indirect" steps, such as removal of a cancerous uterus or an ectopic pregnancy. These acts are not seen as directly intended to kill the fetus; its death is an indirect, unintended result of an act with a "double effect." Callahan writes:

> When one or more human beings refuse to save the mother by the 'murder' of the fetus, she is being refused by other human beings the *de facto* right to life; her rights are nullified. To say that 'all morality' would be destroyed 'by the killing of the weaker party' is only possi-

ble if one presumes that 'morality' consists in observing moral law regardless of the consequences for individual human beings. The range of human responsibility is thus narrowed to a point where the good conscience of those who could act and the abstract demands of the law take precedence over every other consideration.[35]

For Callahan and many others who reject the strict anti-abortion position these "other considerations," the messy, circumstantial facts of health, finances, stamina, obligations, relationships, and hopes—all the inelegant dailiness of daily life —must weigh heavily in the decision. "When the dilemmas that characterize men's lives are the focus of moral reasoning," Harrison believes, moralists have found ways to overcome this tendency to abstraction. "Over the centuries, Christian moral theologians have wrestled with the question of the use of violence in war—the so-called just-war issue, and in the process they have demonstrated a remarkable capacity for empathy toward the dilemmas of choice that rulers face in war."[36] Only in the dilemmas of women, she believes, have concrete considerations carried so little weight. She and Callahan agree with Gustafson, who says that "specificity of good and evil is the human condition (I never know either in the abstract); choices are agonizingly specific."[37] No one terminates pregnancy in general, but rather this pregnancy, fathered by this man, at this time in this life, carried by this woman, who works at this job and loves these people. Callahan arrives at his position painfully, reluctantly, even regretfully, after frankly admitting that he started out to write a defense of the pro-life position. But, he notes, "It is possible to imagine a huge number of situations where a woman could, in good and sensitive conscience, choose abortion as a moral solution to her personal difficulties."[38]

But one senses that he almost wishes this weren't so. The view he is ultimately forced to adopt admits so many dark and anguishing possibilities that in the end Callahan's line of reasoning only brings us back to where we started and the Supreme Court left us, namely, abortion as a matter for the individual conscience. And the great moral price of freedom is that decisions made by individual consciences are only as good as the consciences making them. This worries Callahan a good deal. He continues, "At the very least, the bounds of morality are overstepped when, either through a systematic intellectual negligence or a willful choosing of that moral solution most personally convenient, choice is deliberately made easy and problem-free. Yet it seems to me that a pressure in that direction is a growing part of technological societies; it is easily possible to find people to reassure us that we need have no scruples about the way we act . . . Pluralism makes possible the achieving of freer, more subtle moral thinking, but it is a possibility constantly endangered by cultural pressures which would simplify or dissolve moral doubts and anguish."[39]

He, for one, rejoices in Rachel's doubts while never denying her the right to make the decision she did. For Callahan too easy a time with this decision might indicate a coarsened conscience. But he might also rejoice with Teresa, that devout Catholic and struggling, devoted mother. She felt the presence of God, she says, throughout the days when she decided on and arranged for her abortion. Indeed, she is sure that only His help made this usually difficult passage so smooth. A great peace came upon her when she knew what she would have to do, and why, and did not leave her as she did it.

"After freedom, then what?" Callahan asks. "Society may have no right to demand that a woman give a good reason why she should have an abortion . . . But this does not entail that the woman should not, as a morally responsible person, have good reasons to justify her desires or acts in her own eyes."[40]

There is probably no decision that one may encounter in the ordinary course of life so deeply personal, so resonant of profound values, so irrevocable, as the fate of a pregnancy. Society, finding no just answer, has left it to the individual conscience, where, in the final analysis, it belongs. Yet we're not fully accustomed to this freedom, nor very comfortable with it.

The moral challenge of the crisis of unwanted pregnancy is precisely deciding this question: "After freedom, what indeed?"

4/

THINKING
ABOUT THE
ALTERNATIVES

"In this world there are only two tragedies. One is not
getting what you want and the other is getting it."

Oscar Wilde

Barbara Radford, director of training and community education at Preterm, a clinic in Washington, D.C., and a counselor
with years of experience in abortion work, recalls the most
difficult case she has ever counseled. A young white couple
came to her office already embroiled in a nasty spat, which
grew into as ugly a quarrel as Radford had ever witnessed.

To spite her partner the woman had gone to bed with a
black man. The pregnancy under discussion may have resulted from that encounter, or may have been fathered by the
white man himself. The decision to abort or not hinged on
the probable race of the baby. "Is there any chance this baby
could be all white?" her partner would ask, taunting the
woman in order to punish her; and she gave as good as she
got.

"They were as verbally racist as anyone I had ever heard
in my life, something I have a great deal of difficulty dealing
with," Radford says. Their reasons, their reasoning, and their

very presence revolted and enraged Radford—plus the fact that the woman "had used the other man to do this. Such horrible things were said—they were horrible—everything about them was so awful for me that it hurt. I mean, telling it now hurts. It was that awful."

And so this despicable woman decided to end her pregnancy on these morally repugnant grounds. Could this possibly have been the right choice?

Radford, who has thought long and deeply about the meaning of abortion in people's lives, answers without hesitation. "Obviously," she says. "They made the right choice for them." And she adds, "I do philosophically believe that people make the best choice for themselves."[1]

By this Radford doesn't mean that everything people decide to do about an unwanted pregnancy is right—that any decision is fine simply because somebody made it. She has seen many, many terrible decisions in the making. And in her years as a counselor it was her job to stop people from making those terrible decisions and help them make better ones; she has helped women decide to abort and helped others decide not to.

What she means is that in her experience ordinary people are capable of arriving at sound judgments about how to proceed, of making decisions that bring positive results in their lives and that still seem valid years later. And, she believes, only a decision that truly comes out of the particular woman's life and experience, wrought by her own mind and heart, can achieve these ends.

But getting there—to a particular choice—is rarely very much fun; indeed, reaching the decision is for many people the single most difficult part of the crisis of an unwanted pregnancy. Of course, the word "crisis" has been badly debased in recent years, cheapened to mean any period of difficulty or stress; but its true meaning, based on its original Greek root, is more exact, and describes precisely the situation of a woman unwillingly pregnant. "Crisis" comes from Greek words that imply both "decide" and "separate"; dictionaries define it as "a turning point for better or worse." It is that small space in time that divides two possibilities; the moment in an illness, for example, when it becomes clear whether the fever will break and the patient live or intensify and the patient die.

For a woman facing an unwanted pregnancy it is the choice between alternate, very concrete futures. She either will or will not give birth seven months from now, at income tax time, say, or the week after Thanksgiving. There is nothing theoretical about it. Although a certain number of miscarriages do occur, in practical terms there are only three possibilities: She will carry to term and keep the child; she will carry to term and relinquish the child for adoption; or she will abort the pregnancy. She must choose one of these. Even declining to choose is a concrete choice, because the pregnancy, if undisturbed, moves inexorably forward and will in due time pass beyond the point of no return.

In the best situations, Radford believes, women "process" their decision through multiple filters of the conscious and unconscious mind. She uses the word in a technical sense to mean working a decision out gradually, or at least over a period of time, until it feels right, until, in other words, there are no unconsidered objections to the proposed plan from anywhere in the conscious or unconscious mind. Radford has seen very different but equally valid styles of decision-making. Some people write actual lists of pros and cons; two columns on a yellow legal pad outline alternate futures and arguments for and against them. Such an exercise can help clarify thinking. "I want a baby," for example, is neither a pro nor a con until the woman understands what she means by those words. Does she want a doll to play with or does she wish to commit herself seriously to nurturing a demanding fellow being? Other people proceed more intuitively, trusting their gut feelings to point them in the right direction.

A good decision takes into account the many people and factors surrounding the woman and her pregnancy. What will it mean to her personal future? Will it enrich her experience or truncate her opportunity for a decent life? Will it condemn her, for example, to an interrupted education, economic insecurity, and welfare dependency?

What will it mean to the futures of those around her, such as parents and other children? Will it require her to stretch her existing resources unacceptably thin? Will it strain or rupture relationships central to her life? Can she meet the emotional and material obligations of parenthood? If she does not already possess the necessary resources, how easily can she assemble them? And what will she have to do to get them? If she does not have this child but wishes to have a child at a later date, will she have a reasonable chance of doing so? How close is she to the end of her childbearing years? How much difficulty does she have conceiving? If she does not wish to raise a child herself, how does she feel about adoption? Would her circumstances permit her to complete the pregnancy and relinquish the child without causing unbearable social difficulties? Can she accept the idea that an adopted child will pass out of her life definitively, and probably forever?

A good decision, finally, takes account of her ethical scruples and her image of herself as a moral person. What does she believe about abortion? What does she believe about the nature of the fetus? What does she believe are her overriding obligations in her present situation?

Effective "processing" also includes talking the decision over, ideally with someone close and trusted who has a clear image of the woman's way of life—often the husband or lover, but possibly a parent, brother, sister, friend, or even a clergy member. "It doesn't seem to matter so much what the relationship is so long as the woman knows it's somebody who cares about her and supports her decision," Radford observes. For women who have no friend or relative to turn to, and even for some who do, an experienced professional counselor can help think things through. Many abortion clinics, especially those with a strong feminist orientation, offer pregnancy counseling; without further obligation a woman or couple can talk their feelings out with a person who has seen many others wrestle with this decision but who has no preconceived notion of the right outcome for this particular case. This distinguishes legitimate pregnancy counseling from so-called "services" generally associated with the right-to-life movement, whose real purpose is dissuading women from aborting. If a woman decides to carry to term, a good clinic doesn't see her as a lost client. "We're delighted," Radford says, "so long as she made the right decision for her."

Making momentous decisions is rarely easy for anyone, and for many women it may be harder still. Not only is the possibility of controlling a pregnancy's outcome new and not completely familiar for many people, but deciding almost anything means exercising control over one's destiny. Many women have been raised to see the exercise of control as difficult, threatening, perhaps even unfeminine. Indeed, in the traditional definition of sex roles passivity and resignation, rather than any attempt to resist or direct one's fate, is woman's lot. (Men do not have a "lot" in that sense; they have "man's estate.") Women may plot or plead to influence the outcome, but in this view of relationships the big decisions—to propose marriage, for example, or to have children—lie outside her control, in a man's hands, or in God's.

Quite beyond the question of femininity, age may play an important part. For girls in their early adolescence, as Radford says, "making decisions is simply not part of their experience." And, beyond that, most young adolescents probably lack the developmental maturity to understand that wishes and magical thinking cannot effect the outcome, that issues of blame and power ought not to be uppermost, and that any decision will have concrete and irreversible results. Even for somewhat older adolescents who have a bit of practice in deciding small questions, making a decision of this size is a wholly new experience; this is very probably the first large decision they have ever taken in their lives.

Very young women represent a disproportionate share of the more complex and costly second trimester abortions for the simple reason that they often take so long to decide; first they evade the reality of the pregnancy, and then they vacillate among possibilities. Tammy, for example, like girls her age, had quite irregular periods, so it took a while before she even realized that hers was overdue. For the next several weeks she considered and rejected the idea of pregnancy because at fifteen she was "too young" and, anyway, she had only "done it a few times." But several more weeks passed with no menstruation, so she polled her girlfriends for methods of "making her period start." When jumping off furniture, carrying friends piggyback, falling down stairs, and lifting heavy cartons proved futile, she asked the several young possible fathers what they thought. Each of them denied involvement, because she couldn't "prove" he was the one. Her jeans were getting tighter and her period still hadn't begun, but Tammy was sure her mother would "kill her" if she knew. When, at last, the mother did confront her with the obvious, Tammy was several weeks into her second trimester.

So the first and most basic step in this decision is deciding to decide at all. Margaret, for example, decided not to. Pregnant with a third, unexpected, child at forty-one, and fully aware of the shortening odds on producing a baby with Down's syndrome at her age, she declined to undergo amniocentesis, which could uncover the presence of the abnormality in time to abort. "What would have been the point?" she asks. "I knew I could never bring myself to do anything about it." A devout Catholic, she had determined in advance that the fate of a pregnancy was simply outside her province of decision. But another woman of similar background, facing a similar threat, might make a different decision about whether to decide. Teresa, for example, whom we met in the previous chapter, decided that she must take her future into her own hands in order to do what she felt to be God's will, namely, caring for her doomed daughter at home without risking a second handicapped child.

These two women, facing the same question and coming from the same religious background, both believe that they made the best—indeed, the only possible—choice. Together they illustrate Radford's credo: People can make their own best decision.

But how do they go about it? In fact, we know very little about what happens to people while they decide for or against abortion, and that in itself poses a real problem for many in the throes of the decision. Insightful counselors such as Radford have personal, empirical understandings of the process, but there's really no accessible "oral tradition" about abortion—as there are, for example, about menstruation and birth—nor even much of a written tradition based on literary insight or social-science research. For women who don't know of a friend who's been there before, there are, in short, few if any reliable and easily available models for how someone in this situation ought to act and feel, and this leaves many adrift on their own seas of anxiety and nameless terror. "I'm not the type of person this sort of thing happens to!" women object, when in historical fact, the unwillingly pregnant are every kind of woman there is. It's just very hard to find that out at the beginning.

"I really love being reduced to a cultural stereotype!" a character in *Annie Hall* sarcastically objected when Woody Allen placed her in her demographic pigeonhole; but, in fact, real people in trouble often do find great comfort in knowing that they're feeling the same things that others in their position have felt. As we know, the feeling of being a deviant—of standing outside the pale of "normal" behavior—is central to most women's experience of abortion and can very effectively cut them off from feelings of connectedness, from the knowledge that they are still fully human and worthy people. "I feel so alone," many women say. Most of Zimmerman's subjects told very few others and tried to keep the knowledge from even some of their intimates. But knowing what others have thought, done, and felt, and what the experience meant to their lives, could, if people only had the information, help them to come to wise decisions with less pain.

Yet, sadly, the really striking thing about the large ex-

isting literature on abortion is how little it tells us about the
actual experiences of real women. Great forests have been
felled to permit authors—usually male—to debate the morality of abortion, but hardly a sapling sacrificed to record what
women have actually undergone. Women trying to learn
from the experience of others thus face a real obstacle: Although tens of millions of living veterans surround them,
very few of these struggles have contributed anything to a
systematic understanding of abortion. Most women don't talk
about their experience in any detail; each person's passage
thus remains an anecdote rather than becoming part of a recognizable and illuminating pattern of adaptation.

When loving advice fails them, people in trouble often
turn next to the colder comfort of books. But even here it is
not easy to find what a woman wants to know. Only recently
have fine, imaginative writers begun exploring abortion as an
experience in itself rather than as an illustration of some
other point. The relatively few works by social scientists and
journalists are, naturally, flawed by their authors' respective
techniques: on the one hand, cumbersome methodologies and
impenetrable jargon; on the other, lack of a theoretical framework to unify disparate, largely unanalyzed cases. A person
in trouble doesn't need intellectual discipline or undigested
emotion, but someone to identify with, someone whose experience can point the way. Even though the existing literature
doesn't make it easy to ferret out, there, behind the footnotes
and headlines, is hidden just such information.

A few authors have recorded the experiences of numbers
of women, and even fewer have subjected those experiences
to analysis that produces insights into what, beyond suffering, is actually going on. Happily, however, these researchers
have come to quite similar—and instructive—conclusions.

Zimmerman's is probably the most thorough study of
the "passage through abortion," following forty women from
the moment they discover their pregnancies to the months
following their abortions. As we have already seen, she believes the central experience is dealing with deviance, finding

the meaning of a highly problematic situation, and fitting that meaning into the other meanings in a specific life. Not all of Zimmerman's group responded alike; indeed, she found that the circumstances of their current lives strongly influenced the women's reactions. Thus, she found something of immense use for every woman facing a problem pregnancy.

But a scholarly vocabulary and format have kept that something hidden from many people who could benefit, so we will examine Zimmerman's findings (and some others as well) fairly closely. The best way to predict an experience is to know how it went for others like you, and that knowledge is what the social scientists provide in often intimidating detail. They provide many clues that people can use to make educated guesses about their own probable futures. The women studied had sufficiently varied backgrounds, beliefs, and styles of thinking so that many kinds of women will be able to say, "Here's what's likely to happen to someone like me."

Zimmerman divided her women along lines of what she calls "affiliation." Those who were "securely rooted or enmeshed in social life"[2] had an easier time than those who were "less firmly attached to their social worlds . . . in flux."[3] The first group, often older and always more settled in their relationships, more established in their adult conceptions of themselves, more sure of their possibilities and aspirations, were "clear about their obligations, expectations, and futures. They knew who they were and where they were going."[4] This knowledge helped make the meaning of their pregnancies clear.

The other women, often younger and always more confused about life generally and their own place in it, had a more turbulent time. Because they had "less sense of purpose than the former group,"[5] they also had more difficulty putting their pregnancies into a larger context based on the overall plan of their lives. They couldn't easily figure out what this new possibility meant because they had no coherent idea of what their lives meant.

Zimmerman doesn't believe that this connection between orderly lives and easier decision-making is accidental. "Affiliation tended to mean that a woman had a definite plan for the future," she writes. "If a baby was not part of this plan, then frequently she viewed her pregnancy situation as providing no alternative to abortion . . . Being affiliated, knowing who she was and where she was going, gave the women a sense of the 'right time' to have a baby."[6]

But a woman whose social circumstances provided few hints about her probable future can't as easily sort out what the pregnancy means in her life. "My parents will throw me out of the house," or "I'll have to quit school," or "I have no money," or "My boyfriend won't help me" are statements of fact, not of social meaning. They only take on social meaning in the larger context of an entire social situation. Each may seem to argue against continuing the pregnancy, but in fact can point in either direction. A woman, for example, might wish to break away from her parents and may welcome an apparently outrageous pregnancy as the means to independence. Or she might hate school and see no purpose in continuing. Or she might want to use the pregnancy to get money (e.g., from welfare). Or she might not need her boyfriend's help because she can count on her family's. Which is which depends entirely on how (and whether) she is tied into her social universe.

The affiliated women appeared to have an easier time for another reason. Having clear, stronger social ties, they knew where to go for help and support. They knew who should be told and whose opinion asked. They had people they could count on and channels they could use to get what they needed, be it hand holding or the price of an abortion. Nearly all the women tried to involve trusted others in the crisis, but the less affiliated women simply had fewer people they could call on, and ironically ended up telling considerably more individuals than the affiliated women, perhaps hoping to find the pregnancy's meaning from a constellation of opinions and advice.

"But wait a minute" you might be thinking at this point. "Zimmerman implies that women decide for or against abortion based on its *social* meaning in a given set of circumstances. What about all that stuff in the last chapter about morality and the rights of the fetus? Doesn't that enter in? Or do women actually make this decision immorally, or at least amorally?"

Like so much else involving abortion, the answer depends on particular meanings. If "deciding morally" means that abstract theological considerations of the woman's rights versus the fetus's rights control the decision, then it's probable that many, even most, women decide for abortion "immorally, or at least amorally." But if "deciding morally" means weighing the ethical issues that appear most relevant to those involved, then abortion decisions usually—perhaps almost always—entail a good deal of moral struggle.

"The more directly an individual is involved in some role of responsibility in the pregnancy," observes Janice Muhr, another close observer of the process of abortion, "the more his meanings rely on the particularity of the experience. Less intimately involved actors—family, friends, acquaintances [and perhaps outside moralists?]—tend to rely more heavily on the stereotyped social meanings of abortion."[7]

And that is so precisely because for most women the "particularity of the experience" *is* its ethical meaning as well, while for most of the moralists who have written on the subject the ethical meaning is something else entirely. Psychologist Carol Gilligan is probably the first to state this difference explicitly and in terms of abortion decisions. Her studies of the moral reasoning of women, described in her groundbreaking book *In a Different Voice*, lead her to the conclusion that, in general, women approach moral problems from quite a different standpoint than most men. Although Gilligan's language is a bit difficult, it is worth hearing her state her central point in her own voice, because she says what she means very exactly.

When one begins with the study of women and derives developmental constructs from their lives, the outline of a moral conception different from that described by Freud, Piaget, or Kohlberg begins to emerge and informs a different description of development. In this conception, the moral problem arises from conflicting responsibilities rather than competing rights and requires for its resolution a mode of thinking that is contextual and narrative rather than formal and abstract.[8]

Gilligan believes that throughout their lives women think about moral problems differently from men. Instead of the masculine conception of morality as a balance of each person's rights (e.g., the fetus's versus the mother's), women concentrate on the realities of need and suffering of each individual involved. The moral solution is thus not necessarily the "fair" one but that which causes the least pain. "This conception of morality as concerned with the activity of care," she writes, "centers moral development around the understanding of responsibility and relationships, just as the conception of morality as fairness ties moral development to the understanding of rules and rights."[9]

The great drama of a boy's psychological development is the separation of his masculine self from the feminine person of his mother; Freud's notion of the Oedipal conflict, for example, concerns the process of establishing a boy's male identity. Thus, to both a boy and the man he later becomes, preservation of the self has to do with maintaining clear lines between self and others, and a clear delineation of each party's rights. For a girl, however, no such separation from the mother need occur; she establishes her female self not by opposing but by emulating her mother. She thus lives her life embedded in relationships and preserves her self by understanding and manipulating their subtleties.

In Gilligan's view men tend to conceptualize moral issues as the conflict of rights, while women see them as the conflict of responsibilities. And, indeed, as we saw in the previous chapter, the descriptions of the abortion dilemma as a "calculus of rights" have been formulated and advanced primarily by men. Those, like "unplugging the violinist," that see it as a tangle of incompatible responsibilities come mainly from women.

Gilligan discussed abortion and other moral decisions at length, and over a period of months, with a small group of women. Very few, she found, viewed these problems as abstract ones of conflicting rights. Where men generally felt comfortable in considering many kinds of moral dilemmas abstractly, women often tried to explore the human reasons that lay behind actions; indeed, they even tended to people hypothetical moral dilemmas with real personalities. One such hypothetical problem, for example, concerned whether a man is morally justified in stealing a drug needed to save his wife's life; men concentrated on weighing the right to property against the right to life. Women tended to concentrate on such "side" issues as why the druggist was so hard-hearted as to make theft necessary in the first place. Only in this way can people "consider the social injustice that their moral problems may reflect and . . . imagine the individual suffering their occurrence may reflect or their resolution engender."[10]

Probably the most complete study of how women apply their own particular principles to arrive at abortion decisions —which factors they weigh and how much weight they give them—was undertaken by psychologist Judith Smetana. She interviewed at considerable length several dozen unwillingly pregnant women who had contacted an abortion clinic; some ultimately aborted and others did not. She concentrated on what they thought about while deciding and how this affected their ultimate decisions. Her book is subtitled *Women's Reasoning About Abortion,* but, more significantly, she titled it *Concepts of Self and Morality.* An abortion decision, Smetana concluded, involves much more than the disposition of a particular pregnancy. It seems to tap into the woman's deepest conceptions of what life—both in general and hers in particular—means, and of the nature of the good and the means of knowing it. Smetana is interested in the sociology of knowledge—how people know what they know, what bases of authority they trust, and what systems of reasoning they employ. In understanding abortion decisions, these considerations proved crucial. "Proponents of the so-called pro-life versus pro-choice positions are arguing fundamentally different issues that have their sources in different systems of social knowledge," she writes.[11] Thus, the way an individual construes the problem—the meaning she gives it—will govern the outcome of her reasoning. And, indeed, like Zimmerman, Smetana found that "an individual acts in accordance with the meaning she ascribes to the situation."[12]

This discovery means that the same act—terminating a pregnancy—can have more than one true, psychologically valid meaning; each of the several possible meanings, in other words, is true and psychologically valid for those who hold it. Abortion can thus be both "murder" and "a woman's right," but rarely for the same person. Many people find this kind of relativity difficult to accept, however; for those convinced about a subject, meanings are clear. According to their respective opponents, for example, people favor abortion because they value convenience above life or oppose it because they wish to prevent women from controlling their own destinies. Proponents, of course, deny such base motives; they know how they see the world, and they know that all right-thinking people see it similarly.

But many—probably most—actual participants enter this crisis without having arrived at *any* clear meaning for the act of abortion. They know that abortion is something not quite nice, and they know that they have a serious practical problem. Apart from that, the great majority of those actually called upon to decide about an unwanted pregnancy have never given the question any serious, concrete thought until their own clock started ticking. In one study of Philadelphia abortion veterans, only 28 percent had "expected to have abortions" if they ever became pregnant; a larger group (37 percent) were "certain they would *never* have an abortion."[13] Of Zimmerman's women, fully 70 percent disapproved of abortion before their own pregnancies; this doesn't mean they opposed the *right* to abortion; rather, they thought it wasn't suitable behavior for themselves. "Approval of the *legality* of abortion does not imply that one approves of the *morality* of abortion," Zimmerman observes. For many women "abortion is considered acceptable under specific circumstances . . . Their own pregnancies do not always fall within these circumstances."[14]

But just where a particular case falls may not be clear until it happens, and neither of the two polar positions on abortion is obviously true except to those attuned to believe it; both, furthermore, become considerably less certain under the stress of actual events. In the words of philosopher Roger Wertheimer:

> The liberal asks, 'What has a zygote got that is so valuable?' and the conservative answers, 'Nothing, but it's a human being so it is wrong to abort it.' The conservative asks, 'What does the fetus lack that an infant has that is so valuable?' and the liberal answers, 'Nothing, but it's a fetus, not a human being, so it's all right to abort it.' These arguments are equally strong and equally weak, for they are the *same* argument, an argument that can be pointed in either of two directions. The argument does not itself point in either direction: it is *we* who point it, and *we* who are led by it. If you are led in one direction rather than the other that is not because of logic, but because you respond in a certain way to certain facts.[15]

Every demographic study of abortion suggests that Roman Catholics, for example, who ought to reject abortion overwhelmingly if the pro-life argument were self-evidently true, account for about the same percentage of abortion patients as they do of the general population. Does this mean several hundred thousand bad Catholics a year? In some cases yes, but in many others decidedly not, at least in the women's own estimation. Indeed, a national pro-choice association called Catholics for a Free Choice claims a sizable membership of active communicants, including nuns and priests. Their interpretation of Church teaching leads them to the conclusion that the individual conscience is the final arbiter of right and wrong and, further—since the Church has never made the ban on abortion an infallible teaching—that the conscience is free to consider an abortion as a moral possibility.

Indeed, Altagracia, a devout Catholic of Latin ancestry, suffered enormously while struggling with two apparently equally unacceptable alternatives: aborting a pregnancy or bringing an illegitimate child into her tightly knit, strictly moralistic family. The pain dragged on for weeks after her abortion as she wrestled with the certainty that she had committed a grievous mortal sin and would surely be punished. Then a friend suggested she have a certain priest hear her confession, and to her astonishment he absolved her. So now she wrestles with an outcome of her moral drama that contradicts everything she thought she knew about sin. "I don't understand how he could do that," she says, "and yet the Church gives him the power." The point is, of course, that any particular decision about abortion is part of a general approach to larger issues.

Smetana found four distinct styles of thinking about abortion "based on fundamental differences in the definition of human life. While all women clearly considered the child a human life at birth, they varied in the judgement about when a fetus should be considered a human being."[16]

"Moral reasoners," who constituted about a quarter of her sample, saw the issue as one of balancing justice between persons. They believed that human life began at conception, and thus their problem was how to weigh reasons for taking a life.

Nearly half the women were "personal reasoners," who did not view the fetus as a separate life but as an "extension of the mother during pregnancy. As a result, abortion is considered exclusively an individual choice, and pregnancy decision making is treated as an issue of control over one's own body, reproductive functions, and life."[17] In their own lives these women make Sumner's distinction between moral issues—those that affect and thus concern other people—and personal decisions, which affect only oneself.

Another quarter of her sample—the "coordinated reasoners"—combined these two apparently incompatible approaches. With Sumner and the Supreme Court they believed that although the fetus started out as an extension of the mother, at some point before birth it crosses the boundary to independent existence. "Characteristically, these women define an equal human life as one that is fully developed and resembles a human form. This point or span of time becomes pivotal in coordinating the moral and personal concerns of abortion."[18] Different people drew the line at different points, and the kind of thinking they did about their personal situation depended largely on whether or not they had passed their own threshold.

About 7 percent of the women, the "uncoordinated reasoners," could find no common ground among competing claims of morality and personal rights, which they saw as mutually exclusive. Confused and vacillating, they reasoned in futile circles, never arriving at a clear resolution.

In Smetana's study "domain of reasoning"—the area that the woman marked out as the scope of her problem—was the single best predictor of how she would ultimately act. Would she, for example, view her decision as one of balancing her rights against those of another being, or of merely exercising legitimate control over her own body? No other factor—personality, age, social or economic position, upbringing, religion, marital condition, or way of life—came even close. Women who aborted were generally somewhat more educated and somewhat less religious than those who didn't, but these factors in themselves weren't particularly reliable predictors. What separated the women was a difference in worldview. According to Smetana,

> While women who chose to terminate their pregnancies do not seem to differ from other women in personality characteristics, they do appear to hold different views toward abortion, pregnancy, and motherhood . . . Positive attitudes toward abortion are one of a constellation of other social factors, including school performance and desired family size, that are associated with the decision to abort a pregnancy.[19]

This "constellation of social factors" apparently relates to particular experiences or notions derived from upbringing. "Age, mother's education, education, religious background, and religious attendance accounted for nearly half the variance in reasoning about abortion."[20] Those with educated mothers, or who had grown up in relatively small families, or who rarely attended church were likelier to view the issue as personal. Catholic versus non-Catholic religion was the single strongest predictor of reasoning style, but, interestingly, religion itself did not determine the ultimate decision. Religion influences action, Smetana believes, by influencing the style of reasoning a woman adopts. Catholics, for example, more often see the problem as moral but "are not more likely to continue a pregnancy than to abort."[21] More educated women were likelier to reason personally and to abort.

Style of reasoning predicted the outcome better than anything else but still did not predict it in all cases. Within their chosen realm of meaning, women continue to negotiate the best course through their own difficulties. A woman who sees abortion as taking a life, for example, may still do so if she believes her reasons pressing enough. According to Smetana,

> Women who consider abortion a moral issue treat the fetus as a life to be weighed in pregnancy decisions. The

value of life varies according to moral judgement stage and can result in either decision, to have the child or terminate the pregnancy. Typically, however, women reason that the preservation of life is more important than the woman's needs in the situation. This results in decisions to continue the pregnancy.[22]

But not always. The pressing issue—and the moral dilemma—can become considerably more complicated if it is defined to include more than the rights of the mother and the fetus. What if the woman defines her problem in such a way that she considers the pregnancy's effect on other people in her world—her parents, her other children, her husband, or lover?

Gail, for example, though not a frequent churchgoer, is the mother of preschoolers. She cherishes early pregnancy, having achieved her first two only after painful and costly fertility treatments. "Once you've given birth," she asks, "how can you believe it's not a life?" And yet, when she found herself unexpectedly pregnant while nursing her new infant, she had to weigh her conviction against the good of her entire family. Various business uncertainties had left their finances shaky; Gail felt severe pressure to return to work as soon as possible. Her husband, facing a crucial time of stress in his career, felt that he could stand neither the additional responsibility nor the extra work of yet another baby. "I love babies," Gail says ruefully, "and I would have liked to have this one, especially after all the trouble I had with the others, but sometimes you have to choose between the pregnancy and your husband." Her responsibility to him and her existing children, so far as she could see, left her no choice.

Although Smetana doesn't explicitly discuss this issue, her results seem to confirm Gilligan's conclusion that a woman's moral reasoning has less to do with rules than with relationships, with what Gilligan calls "a responsibility to discern and alleviate the 'real and recognizable trouble' of this world."[23]

Any woman who can recognize herself in one of Smetana's subjects now knows what many others like her have done. And Gilligan's work carries a bracing message of cheer for perplexed women: "Trust your own moral instincts," she seems to be saying. "Moralities you read or hear preached may not reflect the issues you think important."

Gail, like most women, dealt with her problem in terms of real personalities and real limitations on time and money, so the solution she settled on was not the solution she ideally would have wished. But, still, it was her own solution, "processed," as Radford says, through her own understanding of her life and her own moral vision. And this, Radford believes, is a crucial distinction.

In many many cases the woman cannot have everything she wants. Any decision carries very real costs. For Bonnie Fritz of Frederick, Maryland, the decision to abort meant a decisive break with her husband Chris. Even before becoming pregnant a second time she had begun to conclude that they had probably married and become parents too young. She simply didn't feel that she could responsibly raise another child in her unsatisfactory marriage. But when she attempted to arrange an abortion, Chris got a court injunction to stop her. Days ticked by while the opposing lawyers filed papers in various courts. Suddenly a brief hiatus between stays appeared to leave Bonnie temporarily free to obtain an abortion—and she did. Chris, however, vowed to take his battle, namely, for the right of the father to prevent an abortion, to the Supreme Court if necessary.

Another wife, Linda, paid a more subtle cost. Like Gail she had a "completed" family; an unplanned "extra" pregnancy; a similarly unwilling husband, Tom, who wanted her to return to work; and nearly as tight a financial bind. They discussed it and decided to abort. She made an appointment at a clinic, and then, at the last minute, cancelled it. "She just couldn't bring herself to do it," Tom recalls, "and I didn't see how I could force her. She's a good mother, with a warm heart, and she felt she would be killing a baby. She felt terrible about 'letting me down,' as she said, and I knew there would be trouble, but I just couldn't force her. It was a losing proposition either way. But, still, if she had been able to go through with it, things might have been better afterwards." Tom and Linda's marriage began to go sour when the new baby arrived. Tom, carrying the whole financial burden, felt ignored and unappreciated as Linda turned her attention to yet another child. His anger and disappointment deepened at seeing the slender, carefree girl he had married turn into a hefty, competent hausfrau who treated him like another of her household tasks. He admits with dismay that he drifted into a series of casual affairs with women at work, one of which became serious enough to threaten his marriage. Now permanently separated from his wife, Tom looks back on the entire episode with regret. He doesn't really blame Linda for the decision she felt she had to make, but for them the costs of his final child were far more than financial.

"It being the woman's decision doesn't mean making a wish list," Radford says. "It means working to find what she can live with." Radford has seen numbers of women on the way to decisions that would have had serious, detrimental, long-term consequences, often ignored or unnoticed by the woman herself. Very young women's lack of worldly experience, Radford thinks, can make them particularly susceptible to unrealistic, even fantastic, planning. Beyond that, Smetana writes, "adolescents do not differ from adults merely in the extent of their social knowledge. Rather they have qualitatively different ways of representing and interpreting the world, processing information, and constructing solutions to the logical, moral, and personal problems they face."[24] Research by the great Swiss psychologist Jean Piaget shows that very few adolescents have reached a level of maturity that permits them to think abstractly and objectively about their own situation.

But, even so, it is important to remember Radford's concern that the decision be the woman's own. Very young women may not think exactly as adults do, but they still need to be allowed to arrive at a resolution they can live with. Even if keeping or terminating a pregnancy means, for example, the end of schooling or a break with spouse and family, it still might be the right choice if the woman chooses carefully —and knows her own mind.

When sixteen-year-old Diane Miller found herself to be a mother in April 1968, she had no money, only a tenth-grade education, and not even the good wishes of her family. "When I called them from the hospital," she recalls, "they called me a whore and a slut. I never cried so bad in my life."[25] And to make matters worse, the baby, Greg, weighed only two and a half pounds at birth and soon was diagnosed as blind. But Diane determined to raise him herself, first living on welfare in a dingy apartment, and then gradually finishing high school, attending college, buying her own suburban home, and seeing her son grow into an intelligent and athletic teenager. By the age of thirty, Diane had become an assistant supervisor in the pathology lab of a world-renowned hospital. Greg—and what she calls her "unrealistic decision to keep and raise him"—"gave direction and meaning to my life."

The point, as Radford sees it, is not to make any particular choice in every such case but to be sure the woman understands the costs of what she chooses. Good counseling, Radford says, "helps them see that they have other things they want and other things they need, and oftentimes those supersede this."

And these wants and needs can vary widely, depending on the woman's personal situation, her cultural background, and the community she belongs to. Not only abortion but also pregnancy, motherhood—and nonmotherhood—have very different meanings in different cultural milieus. From her discussions with dozens of women, journalist Linda Bird Francke concludes, "Middle class white women tend to abort their first pregnancies and to deliver later ones, while women of lesser financial and educational means tend to deliver their first pregnancies and to abort subsequent ones."[26] Psychologist Janice Muhr's study of how women adapt to abortion uncovered striking differences in values that explain this strikingly divergent behavior. For white middle-class women motherhood is a perfectly acceptable role in the right circumstances—those that do not interfere with middle-class respectability and living standards. And these concerns involve far more than "immoral" or "amoral" concerns with status or comfort; they define a woman's "moral" responsibility to provide a "decent" upbringing—one that offers the child opportunity and respect in its mother's world.

For poorer, especially urban black, women, on the other hand, motherhood may be the only acceptable—or even imaginable—role for an adult woman, "with or without the structure of the 2-parent family to support this role. Sex outside of marriage is generally accepted, if not expected, and single motherhood is commonplace. First pregnancies are rarely aborted."[27] Indeed, in such a community aborting a first pregnancy may well constitute a break with family values and a step up the ladder into the middle class. But if motherhood is a central feature of adult identity, so is the need to "do right" by the children. Poor women who find later pregnancies threatening their more modest aspirations for their existing children often turn to abortion.

The most typical abortion patient in the United States, an unmarried, middle-class white young adult without children, aborts to preserve entirely different values. "Small family size," "disapproval of single motherhood," and "increasing sanctions for multiple roles for women" generally permit —and often compel—a decision for abortion. "The moral imperative at work here on a society level is focused not on abortion," Muhr writes, "nor even on sexual activity, but on the need to maintain cultural propriety regarding family structures."[28] Evelyn, a suburban high school senior, aborts because her pregnancy might "ruin" her life. It would force her to take a low-paying clerical job instead of starting at the reasonably select college she might otherwise expect to attend on partial scholarship. It would certainly spell the end of her dream of attending a top law school. LaVerne, on the other hand, sees no such threat. Could she ever qualify for the clerical job Evelyn disdains, it would represent a vast improvement over the chaotic life her parents have led in a teeming city slum. Her life, in Evelyn's sense, was "ruined" before she was born. But Evelyn's decision certainly isn't a question of not wanting children but merely of not wanting to carry *this* pregnancy to term now. Under 40 percent of Zimmerman's women didn't want a baby—sometime, only not this baby, and not now.

Indeed, some of the very saddest and most difficult decisions come in the cases when both mother and father do want a baby very badly but decide that this baby must be aborted. Pauline and David, for example, rejoiced when, after months of frustrating, humiliating, and painful fertility treatments, they finally conceived their much-desired baby. But amniocentesis showed that, both being carriers, they had passed on the fatal, genetically transmitted infantile Tay-Sachs disease, a disorder of the nervous system that kills painfully and without fail by age four. With her first pregnancy aborted in midtrimester, and a one-in-four chance of conceiving another Tay-Sachs baby, Pauline wonders whether she has the strength to face months of fertility treatments to try again.

But for Sylvia medicine's new power to detect genetic disease in the womb is nothing but a blessing. "If they had had that when I needed it, I certainly would have married him and had the baby," she says, thinking of her pregnancy over twenty years ago. A career woman in her late thirties, Sylvia conceived by a married man, her partner in a passionate affair. "He offered to divorce his wife, but I was afraid." A family history of disease, along with what was then considered her advanced age, convinced Sylvia that the genetic risk was too great; her doctor arranged a "therapeutic" abortion on fictitious psychiatric grounds.

When Susan married her second, childless husband—

they were both in their mid-thirties—she thought she knew how pregnancy "ought" to feel; she had borne a son in her teens. Though still just below the cutoff age of thirty-five, she had a persistent "funny feeling" about her second pregnancy and insisted on amniocentesis despite her doctor's assurances that it wasn't needed. Sure enough, her intuition was right: Down's syndrome. She aborted this pregnancy by the traumatic saline instillation method, and another one for the same reason and in the same manner, before she presented her husband with his much-desired firstborn.

Although the actual process of decision-making may be easier in these cases (after all, the women fulfill all of Zimmerman's requirements for an "affiliated" woman), the psychological pain is nonetheless often very severe. Amniocentesis must wait until after the sixteenth week. By then the pregnancy has both a psychic and social reality; the parents have passed into the phase of "we're having a baby." One study found that "depression, guilt, and self-reproach" were more common in genetic cases than in abortions "for psychosocial indications."[29] Guilt revolved not around the appropriateness of continuing this pregnancy but the apparent inability to produce a normal family at all.

Indeed, when Zimmerman wrote that some women have an *easier* time, she didn't mean to imply that they have an easy time, a decision without strain. One woman spoke for many when she said, "I knew what I had to do and I was dead set on doing it, but I didn't want to . . ."[30] Nearly everyone feels some ambivalence, some conflict, over so large and grave a decision. For example, Joanne, a devoted feminist, astonished herself; firmly convinced of her right to control her own body, she expected an abortion to be a rather routine medical experience. When, however, a casual encounter with an old friend left her with a pregnancy she could not imagine carrying to term, her previous expectations melted away before a depth of sorrow and regret that had no place in her theory. She believed the abortion necessary and justified. "I only hoped I'd have the strength to go through with it," she says of the days she spent waiting for her appointment. But in the end, she believes, she was one of the lucky few; she miscarried with only a day or two of waiting left. And again she amazed herself: She felt an overwhelming gratitude for her "escape"; she calls this her first religious feeling in years.

But experienced observers don't consider moderate ambivalence any reason not to go through with an otherwise suitable abortion, any more than it's a good reason not to marry, buy a car, or change jobs. "Anytime you make a good-sized life decision," Radford observes, "ambivalence usually precedes it and follows it, too." Indeed, from his exhaustive reading of the literature of abortion, sociologist Henry P. David concludes, "There is no psychologically painless way to cope with an unwanted pregnancy."[31] If the pregnancy is truly unwanted, then carrying to term, followed by raising a child or relinquishing one for adoption, will mean pain as well.

How can a woman best face this crisis, this moment of separating and choosing? How can she find her way among the moral and practical arguments for or against various courses of action? She must attempt to understand what the pregnancy and its possible outcome mean in terms of her own values and her own life. How will they affect her day-to-day life now, next week, seven or eight months, and even years hence? How will they affect those around her? And what will they mean in terms of her self-image and what she values in her life?

As in all crises, trusted confidantes can help. Confidence based on love—that of a spouse, lover, relative, or friend—may mean the most, but confidence based on professional skill—that of a trained counselor—is often a powerful substitute. The crucial requirement seems to be finding a confidante who respects the woman enough to accept the decision she arrives at but cares enough about her to show her its flaws. Beyond that, the work of finding the meaning of the situation is her own. It may not be an easy journey, but the experience of many others shows that if she looks honestly both within herself and at those around her, she can find a direction that, although not perfect, will point her toward the rest of a life she wishes to lead.

5/

TECHNIQUES
OF ABORTION

"The ceremony of innocence is drowned."

W. B. Yeats

Catherine and Barbara both had abortions. Each chose a locally respected medical facility and used a well-trained gynecologist highly regarded by his colleagues. Catherine lay for eleven minutes on an examining table in a small yellow room, looking up at a ceiling covered with stenciled butterflies. She shivered slightly as the doctor slid a cold instrument shaped like a duck's bill into her vagina, and then winced a bit at the stab of pain accompanying an injection. She felt him move instruments in and out of her vagina, and then for several minutes she listened to the drone of a small-appliance motor mingling with the voices of the doctor and nurse as they explained what was happening. Moderate cramps gripped her lower abdomen for a bit. Then the doctor said, "How do you feel? You can sit up when you want to." Surprised, Catherine asked, "You mean it's all over?"

Barbara went to her local hospital in the morning and was taken down a gray-green corridor to a small examining room, where the doctor met her. Lying on a table in the white room filled with stainless steel equipment, she felt a sharp prick as he gave her an injection in the abdomen, followed only by numbness as he next penetrated it with a much longer needle. An injection from a second long needle produced not pain but a feeling of pressure. "I'll look in on you tomorrow," the doctor said, nodding to the nurse to take Barbara to her room.

She was put to bed in a semiprivate room on a floor full of women, some beaming as they strolled past the big window where the newborn babies were kept, others preoccupied with the operations they would soon undergo for cancer or infertility. There was no one in the other bed, and the room was quite a ways down the hall and around a corner from the nursing station. Barbara looked through magazines and watched a bit of TV. The hours passed slowly because she didn't feel sick, and her worry about what was coming made them even longer. Finally, as the lunch trays were being collected, she felt the first pain, a dull tightening of her lower abdomen. It subsided, but after a while it returned, a bit stronger it seemed to Barbara. The pain came and went, and so did the nurse. During the afternoon she strapped Barbara's arm to a small board, pushed in a needle, and attached it to an intravenous bottle hanging from a pole. By suppertime the pains were more frequent and quite intense, but the nurse didn't stop by as often; the shifts had changed and there were fewer nurses on the four-to-eleven. The evening passed in a gradually increasing crescendo of rhythmic pain. Barbara asked for medicine, but the tablets she took didn't seem to do much good. Before she went off duty the evening nurse checked Barbara over. "It won't be too much longer," she said.

The night nurse, virtually alone on the floor until 7 A.M., looked in shortly. Barbara was panting and distracted by the pain, but she thought she saw a look of distaste cross the nurse's face for just a moment as she considered the night that lay ahead. The pains were very bad now and coming very quickly. The nurse gave her more pills. "I've got to look in on another patient," she said. "I'll be back in a few minutes. I don't think anything will happen right away." But just as the door closed it seemed to Barbara that the pain burst into almost more than she could bear. Panting and sweating, she felt something move inside her, and then suddenly there was a wet, clammy mass between her legs. "Nurse," she moaned, too exhausted to move and too terrified to raise her head and look. "Nurse, help me!" It seemed like an eternity, but it could only have been a couple of minutes before the nurse was there, leaning over the bed and wrapping the thing in a towel. Again Barbara saw the look of distaste—this time she was certain—as the nurse picked the parcel up. "We'd better get you ready," the nurse said. Then Barbara was placed on a table with wheels and was rolling down the corridor to yet another small room. With her eyes closed against the glaring light shining directly on her, she lay on yet another table while a doctor she had never seen before—a young resident whose foreign accent took more concentration to understand than she could muster—gave her more injections and then worked in her vagina with a cold instrument. "There, we have it all," he said to the nurse—a different nurse—in his strange lilt. "Yes, doctor," she said, and wheeled Barbara back to the door. Another ride down the gray-green corridors took her back to her bed, where Barbara fell into a heavy, exhausted sleep.

She woke to find her own doctor, the one she had seen yesterday morning, leaning over her. "Well, Barbara," he said, "How are you? I hear that everything went just fine last night."

"You mean it's finally all over?" Barbara asked wearily.

Between them Catherine and Barbara lived through the alpha and omega of modern abortion experiences, the best and worst treatment commonly available in America today. Catherine's vacuum aspiration was quick, relatively painless, and "safer than normal childbirth"; Barbara's saline instillation was arduous, excruciating, and "more dangerous than a forceps delivery."[1] Moreover, Potts, Diggory, and Peel feel "it is misleading that the two different categories are known by the same name 'abortion.' "[2]

"Abortion" is not the name of a specific medical procedure but of an intended result, the "expulsion of a fetus from the womb before it is viable," according to Webster's New World Dictionary. This desired end can be achieved in a number of ways, depending on the situation. Of these, three basic methods are common in the United States today. The one chosen for a particular woman will depend both on her physical condition and her awareness as a consumer of medical services.

From a technical standpoint, an abortion requires overcoming the features of the female body designed to nurture and protect the pregnancy. The pregnant uterus, though a strong, muscular organ, is lined with soft tissue fed by innumerable small blood vessels. As the pregnancy advances, the so-called "products of conception" become more troublesome to remove: The fetus becomes larger and harder as the bones develop, the placenta more deeply embedded, and the uterine wall softer.

Guarding the entrance to the uterus is the cervix, a tight, hard band of muscle that opens naturally at birth but resists stretching at other times. Beyond that lies the vagina, containing many bacteria that could cause infection in the wrong place or in the presence of damaged tissue. Poking about in the uterus can damage the lining, or endometrium, rupture the uterine wall itself, or damage the blood vessels. Failure to remove all the products of conception can mean severe infection, as can the introduction of vaginal bacteria into the uterus; the rich uterine lining provides a superb medium for the growth of microorganisms.

A successful abortion therefore requires detaching the placenta from the uterine wall and getting it, the fetus, and the other products of conception past the cervix and down the vagina, all without doing any damage to the woman's organs. There are two main approaches to accomplishing this: entering the uterus to remove the products of conception mechanically or inducing the body to go into premature labor. In either case the possible pitfalls are many. Forcibly opening the cervix can permanently harm this crucial muscle, which in a future, desired pregnancy must remain tight to prevent miscarriage; improper dilation can cause a condition called cervical insufficiency, in which the cervix fails in advanced pregnancy, causing the loss of a perfectly normal fetus. It then becomes difficult or impossible for the woman to carry to term without special treatments. In addition, substances used to induce labor can end up in the wrong place or can themselves be toxic. The gynecological wards of hospitals used to provide a living catalog of what can go wrong in abortions: infections, hemorrhages, retained placentas, perforations, shock, gangrene, cervical wounds, injuries sometimes leading to hysterectomy or even death.

But despite—and, ironically, because of—its grisly past, abortion, whatever the type, is now a very safe medical service. Like all surgery, of course, it carries some risk, but according to Curtis Boyd, M.D., a pioneer in providing abortion services, "abortion is now one of the most perfected procedures in medicine." In the United States today fewer than two first-trimester abortions in one hundred thousand end in death; in even the most dangerous procedure, induction with hypertonic saline, there are about thirty-five deaths per hundred thousand.[3] A strange sort of double standard deserves credit here. Because legalized abortion is so controversial and its detractors so alert for reasons to denounce it and dissuade women from choosing it, its proponents have always striven for the very best safety record possible. At first they merely argued that legal abortion would be safer than illegal abortion; now they can confidently state that the type usually performed today, the vacuum aspiration, is a good deal safer than its primary alternative, carrying a pregnancy to term. It is even markedly safer than a tonsillectomy, formerly considered an innocuous procedure that children underwent routinely.

This admirable state of affairs, however, did not arise from a concerted effort on the part of the medical community. Unlike many other modern advances in surgery, most developments in abortion technique occurred not in prominent American medical centers or among prominent mainstream physicians. Rather, medical mavericks coalesced a scattering of observations and inventions on the outer boundaries of the profession into today's safe, cheap, effective first-trimester procedure.

In keeping with their profession's pivotal role in anti-abortion legislation, many members of the medical community felt, and still feel, quite ill at ease with the ethics and technology of abortion. Dr. Boyd's trouble getting into a county medical society may be extreme, but it is not an atypical American experience. In abortion work generally, Boyd believes, doctors feel "more isolation from support systems" than they encounter in other types of services. "You don't have the support you usually do." Dr. Nathanson also recalls the rebuffs he encountered from his professional peers, even in so liberal a scientific bastion as Manhattan. As a group, doctors have always been socially conservative and patriarchal. Potts, Diggory, and Peel observe that "the combination of medicine with anything concerning sex appears to have a particularly paralytic effect upon human resourcefulness."[4] The general culture's image of propriety profoundly affects what physicians believe is safe. In Asia and the Eastern bloc, for example, where Western religious and social notions play no part in public debate, medical attitudes toward abortion have taken quite a different turn. Indeed, Potts, Diggory, and Peel note the following:

> To the student of abortion, the biggest contrast between countries is in medical attitudes, and not in cultural differences dividing populations. It is hard to find a Russian or Japanese doctor who can be convinced that the oral contraceptive is as safe a method of contraception as early abortion. In fact, over a reproductive lifetime, control of fertility by the Pill or by repeated early abortion would appear to be about equally safe. Conversely, few American or British doctors would be happy to consider

the two techniques solely from the point of view of effi-
ciency and medical hazards.[5]

It's not surprising, therefore, that the basic technology
that made early abortion quick and safe and, consequently,
mass abortion feasible came from some unlikely places. Although abortionists have used a variety of techniques for
countless centuries, the forerunners of modern vacuum aspiration appeared about 140 years ago. In 1842 a French physician named Joseph Récamier introduced uterine curettage
(from the French *curer*, "to cleanse"), the practice of scraping
the inside of the uterus with a spoon-shaped instrument
called a curette. In 1874 the procedure was adopted in Ger-
many, then the world center of medical research, and spread
around the world, until the D & C (dilation and curettage)
became one of the commonest operations done on women.

At about the same time an Edinburgh obstetrician, Sir
James Young Simpson, described his use of a vacuum extraction method (exploiting the principle behind the vacuum
cleaner) for "bringing on menstruation."[6] He used a syringe
to create the vacuum, as did the Russian physician Bykov,
who "rediscovered" the method in 1927. After an initial success there, it again passed out of use until "the most recent
rediscovery of vacuum aspiration . . . by Wu and Wu in
China in 1958. Many Japanese doctors had worked in China
during World War II and seem to have known the method
. . . Certainly by the late 1950s and early 1960s it had spread
to Japan, to Russia, and to eastern Europe."[7] It gained particular prominence in Japan, where abortion played a major role
in the postwar drive to control population. However, American and Western European doctors—generally suspicious and
disdainful, if not completely ignorant, of Eastern medical developments—paid little attention until 1967, when Kerslake
used it in Britain. Within a few years it accounted for a third
of all abortions in Britain.

Still, mainline American physicians did not follow suit,
in part because abortion was generally available in so few

places and also because it still lay under an ethical and legal cloud. Standard medical practice for early abortion remained the D & C, in which the cervix is opened and the uterus manually scraped with a curette. This procedure had two advantages. Since it was very familiar—doctors knew it from medical school as the answer to a number of female complaints—no new technique used especially for abortion had to be learned. In addition, a certain number of patients could be "bootlegged" into hospitals for the D & C with the real purpose disguised or left vague.

But there also remained a technical drawback to the vacuum machine; the hard tips, or cannulas, then in use required a fair degree of skill on the part of the operator to prevent perforations, and their thickness required painful dilation. Experimental soft cannulas tended to collapse under pressure, and narrow ones tended to clog with tissue. In the late 1960s, however, the answer came from Harvey Karman, a Californian whom Potts, Diggory, and Peel delicately describe as an "extralegal" practitioner.[8] He developed a narrow, soft cannula with two openings; it didn't collapse or clog and permitted early abortions with minimal dilation. "Not being conditioned by a formal medical training," Potts, Diggory, and Peel observe, Karman "approached the problems of abortion with an open mind."[9] Uppermost was his need to do bearable abortions without an anesthetic, which Karman, lacking medical education, could not safely administer. So when a Chinese-model suction machine fianlly came into use in the United States in 1970, abortion with minimal anesthetic was now safe and mass outpatient abortion possible.

The first step in obtaining an abortion is determining the length of the pregnancy, which in turn will narrow down the technical possibilities. The longer the pregnancy has lasted, the larger will be the products of conception, and thus the wider the cannula and the greater the dilation required to remove them. Dilation is both a technical challenge and the major source of pain during first-trimester abortion; the cervix is a very strong muscle; in teenagers and those who have never had a child it can be quite hard. A menstrual history and pelvic examination will usually suffice to determine the stage in early pregnancy, but past the first trimester a sonogram is necessary to accurately determine the fetus's size.

If a pregnancy, like Catherine's, has not progressed beyond twelve menstrual weeks, then the abortion will closely resemble hers. Severals shots of a local anesthetic will be injected into the cervix. Then, if necessary, the doctor will begin dilation using a set of metal rods of graduated widths. Beginning with the narrowest, each larger one will be inserted and withdrawn until the desired degree of dilation has been reached. The deciding factor is the size of the fetus, as determined by the length of gestation; the greater the tissue that must be removed, the wider the necessary cannula. In some cases, and in some medical practices, other dilation procedures may be used. Sticks of a special dried Japanese seaweed, called laminaria tents, have been found to expand the cervical opening as absorbed moisture gradually causes the laminaria itself to expand. Other clinics may use osmotic dilators, which are laminaria-like sponges, or they may administer prostaglandin, a substance known to relax the cervix, to help in dilation. These methods take a good deal more time, however, and are thus used relatively rarely in the first trimester.

After completing dilation, the doctor places the proper size cannula, which is attached to the vacuum machine's plastic tube, into the uterus and switches on the machine. Manipulating it carefully, the skilled operator empties the womb. An educated sense of feel and a change in the motor's whine usually announce when the process is complete. During these few moments the woman may experience period-like cramps, nearly always quite bearable. A visual check of the extracted material usually tells an experienced operator whether manual curettage is necessary to catch anything missed. If necessary, this procedure follows. Within moments, however, the woman is usually ready to sit up, dress, and complete her recovery in an adjacent recovery room or lounge, where a nurse will check her vital signs, offer her a snack, and administer any needed additional pain medication.

Although the standard abortion with local anesthetic may expose the patient to a bit more pain than is common in American outpatient procedures, nearly all authorities strongly prefer it to the alternative, general anesthesia. Locals avoid the additional risks, cost, and longer recovery time inherent in any use of a general anesthetic. In addition, in the particular case of abortion, there are special benefits. "The use of deep anesthesia," Potts, Diggory, and Peel note, "can result in loss of uterine tone and of the reflex contracticity which normally occurs when the conceptus has been wholly or partially removed and heavy bleeding may result."[10] In addition, other authorities note that this loss of tone makes perforation more likely.

There is, in short, no good medical reason for general anesthesia in suction abortion. But, as counseling experts Carole Dornblaser and Uta Landy observe, there might be other good reasons.

> [Some] women fear pain more than anything else. They are frightened by the idea of an injection. They don't care about risks, safety, and cost as long as they are spared any kind of discomfort. In addition, some may feel emotionally depressed about having an abortion. They may feel guilty or angry about the decision, especially if they are forced to go through with abortion by circumstances beyond their control. So for them, having general anesthesia offers a way of sleeping through the abortion, not dealing with it or facing the reality of it.[11]

Other approaches to pain also exist. At their Fairmount Center in Dallas, for example, Dr. Boyd and his wife Glenna, a professional counselor, have developed a flexible pain management program that employs relaxation and a positive mental attitude, in addition to medication when necessary, to produce a positive experience for the patient. An abortion is a

deeply personal moment and pain a deeply personal sensation, strongly affected by one's emotional state and expectations. Good abortion facilities encourage each woman to
weigh the risks and benefits of various methods of pain control and choose the one that best meet her own needs.

Catherine's abortion represents the best current medical
thinking, but Barbara's does not. Still, the induction or instillation method remains the traditional, and probably the commonest, answer to the problem of a pregnancy that has gone
past the threshold of the second trimester. By *instilling* a toxic
substance that kills the fetus, a doctor can *induce* the body to
begin labor prematurely, thus expelling the dead fetus and
the afterbirth.

Saline abortions, amniocentesis, and other procedures
that depend on locating and driving needles into the amniotic
sac surrounding the fetus must wait until that sac has reached
sufficient size, at about sixteen weeks. An instillation procedure, therefore, often means several anxious, stressful weeks
between diagnosis and procedure; this adds not only to the
psychological pain but also to the danger of this singularly
unpleasant experience. The three weeks that Barbara waited,
for example, not only multiplied her anxiety but doubled her
danger. "Anything that contributes to delay in performing
abortions increases the complication rates by 15 to 30% for
each week of delay," write Willard Cates and David A.
Grimes, experts in the statistical safety of abortion.[12]

In the past women sometimes went home after the first
stage of the procedure, enduring the waiting, pain, and even
the delivery alone. Today, however, instillation abortions almost always take place entirely in hospitals, requiring a stay
of at least twenty-four hours and sometimes up to three days.
This adds considerably to the total expense.

The procedure itself begins when the physician with-
draws a small quantity of amniotic fluid by means of a special
long needle passing through the woman's anesthetized abdomen. This is amniocentesis, the same procedure used to ob-

tain material for diagnosing genetic irregularities in the womb. Replacing the fluid with a substance toxic to the fetus, usually a salt solution but sometimes urea, soon kills it, and after a while labor begins. Some doctors may also use prostaglandins instead of or in addition to saline, or perhaps laminaria, to begin dilation or drugs to speed up contractions.

Induction techniques, though reasonably safe, still carry considerably more danger than suction. The saline solution is toxic to the woman as well as to the fetus, and if it ends up somewhere it doesn't belong, such as in her bloodstream, it can kill her as well. Indeed, misplaced saline causes most of the fatalities associated with this procedure. Prostaglandins avoid this risk but generally produce very unpleasant side effects, such as severe nausea, vomiting, and diarrhea. As Potts, Diggory, and Peel observe, prostaglandins contract "the gut as well as the uterus." They can also contract the small breathing tubes, causing harsh coughing and choking fits. And the earlier the woman is in the pregnancy, the higher the necessary dose and "the worse the side effects."[13]

None of these alternatives is ideal; each substance has serious medical drawbacks. Choosing one requires weighing alternative risks. Prostaglandins have their strong proponents, but the research picture on their safety and efficacy remains unclear and opinion is still sharply divided. Potts, Diggory, and Peel feel that "the real issues generated by developments in prostaglandins may be more in attitudes than in clinical research."[14] They continue:

> Neither urea nor prostaglandins have found much favor in America, where the induction of late abortion by hypertonic saline is still preferred, despite greater dangers. The reason is probably that the less toxic alternatives are more likely to produce an abortion where the fetus may show some signs of life . . . [which are] not only aesthetically offensive, but also [raise] ethical questions.[15]

A fear has haunted this field for years, namely, that of reenacting the sad spectacle of Dr. Kenneth Edelin, brought to trial for manslaughter in Boston for failing to save the life of an aborted fetus inadvertently born alive.

And, indeed, the whole issue of fetal death weighs heavily on the minds of the nurses who must actually attend the delivery, handle the fetus, and thus bear the saline abortion's burden of sorrow. A fetus at sixteen weeks is fully formed and recognizably human; it differs from a full-term baby mainly in size. It differs from a premature infant of the same age, who will be rushed to the intensive care nursery for heroic intervention, in nothing but "the fact that one mother wants it saved and the other doesn't," observes Susan Pasco, R.N., who has attended both types of deliveries in her career as a gynecological nurse.

But the instillation abortion—the willed death of a tiny fetus—radically violates the training and sensibilities of many nurses, who view themselves as laboring for the cause of life. Nurses like Pasco, who provide sympathetic support during the grueling hours of waiting and at the delivery itself, generally do so out of deep commitment to feminist ideals of reproductive freedom. "I believe every woman is entitled to the best care possible," she says, and is willing to endure difficult and trying situations to provide it. Indeed, a strikingly high proportion of the nurses active in abortion work share Pasco's dedication to women's freedom to control their reproduction. Many draw strength from cruel abortion experiences in their own pasts—like the hospital nurse who landed in a strange city's gyn ward after a botched illegal; or the clinic nurse who had to hunt up an abortionist after her husband abandoned her and she needed to go back to work to support her children; or the health educator who, in desperation, aborted herself with the proverbial coat hanger during her student days. "I had such a terrible time," one woman says. "I just want to make sure that no one has to go through what I went through."

But women undergoing salines cannot count on having

such a staunch ally at their side during the long hours of travail. They cannot know whether they will have to endure, along with the pain and anxiety, the palpable disapproval of their most intimate medical attendant. Most suction abortions happen in clinics staffed by doctors and nurses who have chosen their line of work. Salines, however, generally happen on regular hospital services staffed by nurses who merely have agreed to care for women, not necessarily abortion patients. Although some hospitals allow nurses to decline to attend such cases, others do not or cannot. The actual delivery occurs an unpredictable number of hours after the instillation, oblivious to hospital shift rotations, personnel shortages, or vacation schedules. Nurses who disapprove— like those who attended Barbara, for example—sometimes find themselves forced to look after women doing something they find extremely distasteful but who still require the most gentle, supportive care. Talking with medical people long trained to handle gore with equanimity, even those committed to abortion rights, one can't help but be struck by the revulsion many express over late abortions. For some it is an almost insoluble dilemma. One devoutly Catholic nurse, forbidden by her hospital's rules from opting out of the shift rotation, routinely faints when a saline delivery is imminent. "We just know we can't count on her then," a colleague says with a rueful chuckle.

For years this painful, expensive, traumatic experience was the method of choice for mid-trimester abortion. Women diagnosed later than the twelfth week were routinely counseled to wait until a "salting out" could be safely done. Until that time the amniotic sac, which surrounds the fetus, is not sufficiently developed to permit amniocentesis. And no vaginal methods were attempted after the twelfth week. The reason always given was that entering the uterus in that way during the second trimester was "too dangerous"; generations of doctors had read that in their textbooks and heard it from their professors. But was it in fact true?

In the early 1970s a small number of doctors began, almost inadvertently, to find out. Sometimes, Dr. Boyd recalls, he would simply err in estimating the fetus's age, or sometimes some feature of the woman's organs would mislead him. So, with a "first-trimester" abortion under way, he would discover that he was in fact dealing with a larger and older fetus than he had expected. He found that he could safely and effectively empty the uterus of these somewhat more advanced pregnancies by an ad hoc combination of vacuum and manual curettage. Eventually he and some other pioneers generalized these experiences into a scientific conclusion.

The twelve-week cutoff point, he believes, represents no real technological or developmental boundary. It is, rather, a psychological frontier, somewhat like the supposedly "unbreakable" four-minute mile before runner Roger Bannister proved that the only real barrier was the belief that it could not be done. By the same token, the twelve-week mark merely demarcates the first third of the thirty-six weeks of a normal or ideal pregnancy; it is, in other words, a heuristic device. "Development," Boyd says, "proceeds week by week," each week bringing gradual changes and none bringing abrupt transformations. Time counts because it warns the physician of what to expect, not because it has any inherent power of its own. A pregnancy at thirteen weeks, therefore, is just a bit different, a bit more challenging to terminate, than it was at twelve weeks, but certainly not drastically so. But this "conventional cutoff" has a very strong hold on the medical mind. "It was just a taboo to enter the uterus through the cervix" after twelve weeks. And when Boyd and others began to report that they had done so successfully, "it was considered heresy, irresponsible, stupid."

Eventually, however, the experience of Boyd and other pioneers coalesced into a procedure known as D & E (dilation and evacuation). Evidence from Britain during the early 1970s confirmed their observations about its safety, but according to Dr. Philip Stubblefield of Harvard it was "largely ignored."[16] Not until 1977—when Grimes, Schultz, and Cates of the Abortion Surveillance Branch of the highly respected Centers for Disease Control in Atlanta presented statistical data proving that the D & E was *safer* than induction techniques—did the aura of danger and irresponsibility surrounding D & E begin to diffuse. But it only began. "The controversy over curettage procedures for midtrimester abortion," Stubblefield wrote in 1982, is second only to the controversy over whether or not abortion should be legal. "Most professors of gynecology and obstetrics in the United States are still of the opinion that curettage performed after 12 weeks is a dangerous procedure."[17]

Though the procedure is controversial and unorthodox, it is indisputably easier on the patient. Very shortly after D & E became available in their area, Nancy Kaltreider, Sadja Goldsmith, and Allan Margolis looked into how its emotional effects compared with the trials of "salting out." Their results were unequivocal. D & E veterans felt that the procedure "went more smoothly and was experienced more as minor surgery. The amnio group noted that the procedure hurt much more than they expected and was experienced more like labor or a loss of a child."[18] Three weeks after the procedure the amnio group felt depression and anger; a quarter reported a "lingering sense of guilt."[19] None of the D & E veterans suffered this emotional aftermath. "The D & E procedure," Kaltreider, Goldsmith, and Margolis believe,

> allows the patient to continue her characteristic pattern of denial and have a smooth psychological course. The amnio procedure, which is often a frightening experience of pain, fetal expulsion, and medical complications, makes more likely a reaction of hostility and depression.[20]

Encouraged by their good medical and psychological outcomes, the small group of innovators continued to perfect the technique and report their results, but they found it very difficult to convince many of their colleagues. And there is more to the resistance than unconsidered taboos left over from medical school. "As the service is provided in the United States," writes Stubblefield,

> amnioinfusion abortion is easiest on the doctor, who only performs the amniocentesis and inserts medication to begin labor. He then departs, leaving the patient and her nurse to cope with the hours of hard, painful labor and the anguish of the delivery of an immature fetus. With the [D & E] procedure, on the other hand, it is the physician who experiences much of the anguish of the actual performance of the abortion, and we suspect that this contributes in no small way to the reluctance of physicians to adopt this procedure and their persistence in rejecting it as dangerous.[21]

Combining suction with manual curettage and extraction, the physician uses forceps, an instrument for grasping and crushing, to hold those fetal parts (often bony by the latter weeks) that the vacuum machine cannot handle, and move them past the cervix. The parts must then be reassembled to assure that none remains inside the womb to fester and cause infection. Dr. Warren Hern and Billie Gorrigan, from their deep experience with the procedure, conclude, "We have reached a point in this particular technology where there is no possibility of denying an act of destruction. It is before one's eyes. The sensations of dismemberment flow through the forceps like an electric current."[22]

This is simply too much for many well-meaning doctors. "Killing a baby is not a way I want to think about myself," says a doctor who will do so by infusion, but not by D & E.[23] Stubblefield and others have been working to develop techniques using wider cannulas, so that suction can take the place of dismemberment in some abortions up to fifteen weeks. But the central issue still remains for physicians who offer D & E up to eighteen, twenty, or even twenty-two weeks. Still, while not denying the repugnance of the procedure to the operating team, Kaltreider and her associates reject the notion that it is morally any different from "salting out":

Ethically speaking, once the difficult decision is made to terminate a pregnancy in the midtrimester, the means of carrying it out do not differ except in relation to the safety and comfort of the patient. We must continue to investigate the best ways to perform this stressful work.[24]

In addition to its aesthetic repugnance, D & E is an exacting, stressful surgical procedure for the operator. Doctors experienced in first-trimester procedures must learn it gradually, advancing week by week as skill and confidence grow. Those who want to learn it often must seek out a colleague to teach them; few formal training programs or medical schools offer instruction. "To get the word out," says Boyd, "you have to go through the process of getting it into medical school teaching, because if a doctor has heard something in medical school, he still knows it twenty or thirty years later."

In addition to the emotional and technical difficulties of the procedure itself, there is the professional difficulty of being—in fact, of building a practice around being—something of a maverick. A doctor who offers D & E, says Boyd, experiences "more isolation from support systems" than his more conventional colleagues. "It carries such risks to their professional reputation," says Boyd, "such medical and legal implications, as well as the reaction of their peers, that the emotional costs they have to pay in doing the work are just too high."

So we see, once again, the high degree of commitment among many of the medical people who choose to do this demanding work, and do it well. "I relate to the woman and not to the fetus," says Boyd. "I came to believe strongly that the woman had a right to decide when and if she would reproduce." Stubblefield believes that making a woman wait

for an infusion procedure at sixteen weeks is "medically in-
defensible."[25] "There is no other choice that requires more
commitment on the part of the physician to reproductive
choices for women," Hern believes. But he does not believe
that such devotion to the patient's welfare should count as
anything extraordinary. "Many tasks in medicine are difficult," he adds simply, "and this is one of them."[26]

So from every standpoint—medical, psychological, financial, even the opportunity to receive care from committed
providers—the D & E is the procedure of choice for any
woman in the midtrimester who can find an experienced
practitioner willing to accept her case. "There is no advantage to saline," Boyd says, and the safety statistics bear him
out.

The evacuation part, an experience usually quite similar
to a vacuum aspiration, takes anywhere from ten to thirty
minutes longer than a first-trimester procedure, but the dilation part precedes it, and that requires an overnight wait.
The doctor inserts laminaria tents to dilate the cervix gradually. "Once laminaria have been inserted, the abortion has
begun," Dornblaser and Landy warn. "A woman should be
very certain of her decision. On rare occasions she will
change her mind after laminaria insertions and request that
they be removed. There is a possibility she will miscarry."[27]

When the woman returns at an appointed time the following day, the cervix should have dilated sufficiently for the
second stage of the procedure to begin. To protect her health
she *must* return without fail; and in the meantime, she must
abide by certain restrictions that safeguard her from the
greatly increased danger of infection while the cervix, the
uterus's natural line of defense, gradually opens. Nothing
must enter her vagina, not tampons, not bathwater, not
douches, not her own finger, not her sexual partner. Furthermore, she may well have pain, perhaps a good deal of it.
"Those who say laminaria is painless," says Dr. Boyd, "have
no experience with it." There is nothing "wrong" with this

pain, and no benefit to undue stoicism, Boyd believes. Her doctor can and should provide pain medication if necessary.

The evacuation certainly takes longer and may involve somewhat more discomfort than a first-trimester aspiration, but many operators still strongly prefer local to general anesthetic. Boyd finds that the conscious presence of the woman helps him retain his dedication to her interest. In addition, a conscious patient often knows well before the doctor when something serious goes wrong, as, for example, when a perforation occurs. And finally, the loss of muscle tone associated with a general anesthetic can cause even more trouble in this trickier procedure.

Recuperation from the D & E generally resembles that from a vacuum aspiration, although cramps may continue somewhat longer, perhaps for an hour or two. The short recovery time makes D & E, with either local or general anesthetic, a perfectly safe and feasible outpatient procedure. No overnight hospital stay means a considerable saving to the woman.

Because D & E is such a demanding procedure, few physicians feel competent to attempt it after about eighteen to twenty weeks. At that point, Boyd says, "availability drops off rapidly." Some, like himself, go to twenty-two weeks, and a mere handful of others to twenty-four. "The D & E doesn't have the clear advantages over the intraamniotic after 24 weeks," he believes. The woman who needs a very late abortion, therefore, as in some cases of genetic deformity, may have no practical alternative to an intra-amniotic procedure. Some physicians, however, aware of the drawbacks of the intra-amniotic methods, are experimenting with *extra*-amniotic approaches to inducing early labor. Dr. Jane Hodgson, for example, reports a procedure used successfully in Minnesota. On the day following laminaria insertion the woman receives a continuous infusion of prostaglandin outside the amniotic sac until the fetus is expelled. Although it has the side effects of nausea, vomiting, and fever, this method does not carry the peril that intra-amniotic injections do, nor does it appear to have an upper or lower time limit. Hodgson considers continuous infusion of prostaglandin superior to a single dose, in part because it lessens the side effects somewhat but mainly because it permits closer calibration to the woman's needs as the labor progresses. This, of course, implies close monitoring of her condition and continuous involvement of the physician as well as the nurse. According to Hodgson,

> That this method may require as much professional attention as a term labor and delivery is not denied, but we believe that the late midtrimester abortion patient deserves the best of medical care and we deplore the often cavalier attitude taken by physicians who perform the intra-amniotic injection for the second trimester patient and then leave her to deliver by herself or with only a nurse in attendance.[28]

This is only one of several experimental methods used in the midtrimester. A number of doctors are exploring this thorny area, and it's likely that various new or modified approaches will appear from time to time. As Dr. Boyd points out, the entire field is really only a bit over a decade old, "very new in the field of medicine. This is very young for any technology." As the number of workers at the frontier increases, so will the amount and range of total knowledge and experience.

In a very small number of cases none of the second-trimester methods discussed proves suitable. Sometimes the woman waits too long or fails to arrange for D & E (or simply doesn't know about it), and then repeated attempts at induction fail to produce labor (some studies show various prostaglandin techniques failing anywhere from 10 to 40 percent of the time). And sometimes other medical conditions rule out instillation. In this case the doctor must fall back on major abdominal surgery, the hysterotomy, or so-called "mini-Caesarean." Practiced for many years before instillation techniques became available, this procedure involves the use of a general anesthetic, a hospital stay of at least several days, all the risk and pain of a large operation, and permanent scarring of the uterus that might require Caesarean deliveries in future births. The surgeon cuts through the abdomen and into the uterus to remove the fetus and placenta. A woman should only permit this drastic step as a rare, truly last resort, when the time limit for D & E has passed, when induction has completely failed, or when competent experts (not merely one's local gynecologist) have ruled out other procedures because of medical difficulties.

Before we leave the technical aspects of abortion, we must consider a procedure that does not, strictly speaking, terminate a pregnancy because it occurs before a pregnancy generally can be known for sure. This, for many women, is the great advantage of the menstrual regulation or extraction, which is nothing more than a very early suction curettage using either a machine or a large syringe to create the vacuum. Performed up to six weeks after the last period and/or two weeks after the time when the next one should have started, it requires very little if any dilation, apart from that occurring naturally when the very narrow cannula is inserted. It also permits the woman to believe she is merely "bringing on her period," as Dr. Simpson strove to do a century ago, rather than obtaining an abortion.

This end run around the conscience might be, in the opinion of some medical authorities, the procedure's only advantage. It has two great disadvantages, according to this view. It has not proven especially reliable in ending pregnancy, and it exposes women who are not pregnant, and do not need abortions, to the small but still quite real risks of undergoing needless surgery. Fully 30 percent of those undergoing menstrual regulation turn out not to be pregnant, and 1.1 percent will suffer complications as a result of the procedure.[29] Furthermore, says Dr. Nathanson, "The true reason for the delay in the period is obscured."[30] Although few late periods involve serious problems, sometimes conditions such as ovarian tumors and endocrine malfunctions show up first in this way. An artificially induced period, therefore, might mask a potentially dangerous situation.

Of the pregnant women, a substantial proportion will require a second procedure when the menstrual extraction does not end their pregnancies. In a study by Brenner and Edelman, success rates of different clinics ranged from 90.1 percent to 100 percent; in some places up to 10 percent of the women therefore required a second procedure.[31] And the earlier the extraction takes place, the higher the failure rate. All women undergoing this procedure therefore need a follow-up visit with a pregnancy test to ascertain that they are indeed no longer (or never) pregnant. If, despite these disadvantages, a woman still wishes a menstrual extraction, Brenner and Edelman advise the following:

> Menstrual regulation should be performed by experienced physicians who have demonstrated a high success rate . . . Although the procedure is relatively simple, the failure rate is often high until physicians have acquired the necessary experience to perform the procedure proficiently.[32]

6/

UNDERGOING
AN ABORTION

Simone de Beauvoir was probably the first prominent author
to write about abortion not as a moral issue, a social problem,
or a policy question but as a lived experience, a palpable,
particular day one must somehow get through. She wrote
decades ago about illegal abortion in France, but with very
slight changes her description still rings true for women today. If for "law" we understand "cultural ideal," then her
famous central paragraph can still help women prepare for
what they will face as the day itself approaches:

> The moral aspect of the drama is more or less intensely
> felt according to circumstances. It hardly comes in ques-
> tion for women who are highly "emancipated," thanks to
> their means, their social position, and the liberal circles
> to which they belong, or for those schooled by poverty
> and misery to disdain bourgeois morality. There is a
> more or less disagreeable moment to live through, and it
> must be lived through, that is all. But many women are
> intimidated by a morality that for them maintains its
> prestige even though they are unable to conform to it in
> their behavior; they inwardly respect the laws they
> transgress and they suffer from this transgression; they
> suffer still more from having to find accomplices.[1]

Beauvoir researched *The Second Sex*, her classic book on women's place in society, mainly through reading and introspection; women did not openly discuss their abortions with inquisitive strangers in those days in respectable France. But Zimmerman, whose research consisted of talking with American women in detail about abortion day and the days leading up to and away from it, came to a quite similar conclusion. It is the woman's "circumstances," she would agree, that determine what the experience of abortion will be. According to Zimmerman,

> Abortion can be a crisis. On the other hand, it does not have to be. The way the abortion is experienced depends largely on the woman's particular roles in her social world, the way she is tied to a social position. It also depends on the reactions of others to her abortion, on the type of facility where she has the abortion performed, and on her perceptions of that facility. In other words, the way the abortion is experienced is very much a product of the situational circumstances of the abortion passage.[2]

Perhaps the most significant finding is that conditions *within the woman's own control* importantly influence what the experience will be. Women, in other words, have choices to make, and these choices can affect even a straightforward medical encounter.

Zimmerman's women mainly obtained their abortions at one of two local clinics. Clinic A, to which most of the blue-collar people were referred, had a run-down city location, meager decorations and many black employees. Although well staffed, fully equipped, and highly regarded medically, it made a seedy appearance. Women had to travel down streets lined with decaying houses to reach an old former school building sitting in a weedy yard. Inside they encountered a cluster of haphazardly furnished and painted rooms occupied by people with little of the briskness and self-importance (and

none of the starchy white uniforms) often associated with
medical personnel. This generally down-at-heel atmosphere
"meshed with a commonly held stereotype of abortion as
dirty and criminal" and reinforced blue-collar people's
greater habitual mistrust and suspicion of medical care generally.[3] The care offered by Clinic A met high professional standards, but Zimmerman believes that the initial disappointment and unease many women felt made at least the early
hours of abortion day more difficult.

Clinic B, on the other hand, occupied a suite in a modern
office building in a good section of town. Women reached it
by elevator from a well-appointed lobby and entered a recep-
tion area furnished tastefully in a modern design. The clinic
gained prestige from its surroundings, and the white-collar
women who were generally referred there immediately per-
ceived it as a legitimate, reputable establishment. Much of
their suspicion and anxiety quickly dissipated.

For the woman choosing an abortion facility, then,
there's an important lesson here: Selecting a facility where
she feels comfortable can make a big difference in how she
feels about the whole experience, and, not coincidentally,
about herself for undergoing it.

"But wait," you may ask, "what do you mean by *selecting*
a facility? Don't you mean *finding* one? Don't people have to
go where they're referred and hope for the best?" The answer, unfortunately, is that many people do just that, but not
because they have to; rather, they accept the first referral or
suggestion offered because they don't know any better. Indeed, the entire notion of consumer satisfaction lies outside
most people's medical experience; most patients don't judge a
doctor's services as they do virtually every other service they
pay for. They may shop around for a garage mechanic, a hair-
dresser, a housepainter, or even a lawyer, but very few people
view themselves as "hiring" a doctor because his or her style
or qualifications appeal to them. Rather, physicians have appropriated to themselves so much social authority that many
patients feel vaguely grateful to be seen briefly, treated with

barely adequate courtesy, and sent a large bill. Consumerism, now widespread in the rest of the economy, has achieved only small, scattered toeholds in medicine. The concept that a patient purchases a service, and thus has the right to select among competing establishments that treat her with the dignity due a valued customer, exists in very few fields of medical practice.

At its best, however, abortion is one of them. As we've already seen, the medical evolution of abortion services was a bit unorthodox; not surprisingly, their social context is as well. Unlike nearly all other kinds of surgery, the common first-trimester procedure usually takes place not in a hospital operating room or a doctor's office but in a special, freestanding (i.e., independent) clinic devoted mainly or entirely to that purpose. And, unlike nearly every other kind of medical establishment, many of these clinics have a distinctly feminist orientation, using doctors who are employees rather than owners and putting into practice the notion that each woman has the right to dignity as she makes her choice and carries it out.

Indeed, assuring that dignity engages these clinics' professional pride; they see themselves as much more than surgical centers. Many of them offer a range of other women's or reproductive health services as well, such as birth control, sterilization for men and women, VD screening, herpes treatment, pregnancy testing and counseling, and general gynecology. They often view themselves as more sympathetic, more patient-centered alternatives to traditional health care organizations. In a few cases hospitals have established special women's clinics that resemble the good freestanding clinics in atmosphere and outlook.

Many freestanding clinics embody an ideology unusual in American medicine; they also grew out of an unusual set of circumstances. According to Nancy Warford, director of the Northern Virginia Women's Medical Center, their origin goes back to the early days after legalization, when many insurance plans excluded abortions, and many hospitals, for this and other reasons, simply refused to perform them (many still do not). A need (and a market) therefore existed for someone who would offer inexpensive, safe abortions. And a technology existed permitting abortion as a mass outpatient procedure. Thus, small, freestanding clinics, often founded and run by people active in the movement for legalization, grew up to offer a service that traditional medical care providers ignored.

The emphasis on low price and accessibility largely remains unchanged. As Warford points out, because many patients pay for the procedure out of their own pockets rather than through their insurance, they know what it costs; thus, "inflation has been much less in abortion costs than in other medical services." Clinics like hers, she says, aim to "make the service as widely available as possible." In trying to do so, they generally emphasize informality and an accepting, supportive environment. The more obtrusive signs of medical authority—white uniforms, "hospital-colored" walls, sometimes even last names—seem out of place. Not all freestanding clinics, of course, subscribe to these ideals and practices; some are quite traditionally oriented. But a woman who can find one that stresses her emotional ease rather than its own authority goes a long way to assuring herself a smoother emotional passage.

Marjorie, for example, had her abortion in a hospital, on her doctor's advice. A veteran of two Caesarean sections, she appeared to her doctor a poor prospect for a safe vacuum aspiration. (Many other doctors, however, would disagree.) She was thus admitted to her local hospital for a relatively rare first-trimester abortion by D & C. Hospital policy dictated a general anesthetic and an overnight stay. It also meant that Marjorie spent her day alone in a hospital room, except for a woman recuperating from a hysterectomy who occupied the neighboring bed for part of the time. She spoke with no one but her husband about the emotional aspects of what she was doing. She wore a hospital gown for the procedure and a nightgown for the rest of her stay. Her doctor, the nurses, and other staff members treated her as if she were, or recently had been, sick. "Hospitals promote the concept of illness," Warford observes. "Clinics promote the concept of wellness."

But Ginger, who obtained an abortion at a clinic much like Warford's, had a less stressful time. She discussed her situation and decision with a sympathetic and experienced counselor before she met the doctor. Except for the moments she actually lay on the table, she wore her own street clothes. Only for those few minutes, in fact, did she occupy a room with "medical" equipment, and even that stood among a display of bright posters. She recuperated for about an hour in a yellow leatherette reclining chair, in a room full of other women who had recently undergone abortions, nibbling graham crackers, sipping Coke, and talking about their feelings and their plans. She left with a ravenous appetite for a late lunch, because her clinic visit had taken all of a long morning.

Despite the panoply of medical equipment at her doctor's command, Marjorie's abortion was statistically less safe than Ginger's. Marjorie's doctor, though a board-certified gynecologist, actually does only a handful of abortions a month; his practice mainly involves obstetrics and infertility. Ginger's doctor, on the other hand, spends several mornings a week at the clinic doing nearly identical, swift, and relatively painless vacuum aspirations. According to Potts, Diggory, and Peel,

> The concentration of a repetitive procedure [like abortion] in the hands of a limited number of well-practiced operators further reduces the hazard facing the patient. Senior gynecologists who perform relatively few abortions may prove a good deal less skilled at this operation, and have a much higher morbidity [i.e., injury] rate and a much higher complication rate than more junior colleagues who are in constant practice.[4]

And, indeed, statistics bear them out. For the types of abortions customarily performed in outpatient facilities (including D & E) specialized clinics have a better safety record than hospitals. For the rare complications that do arise, a responsible clinic always has hospital backup nearby and a plan for transferring patients to the emergency room in a matter of minutes.

A wise woman chooses an abortion facility in the spirit of a careful consumer. This attitude is especially crucial for second-trimester procedures. She nearly always has some time between diagnosis and deadline to shop around a bit: ask friends, make phone calls, even visit some clinics to find one that not only has a reputation for good services but "feels" right. All reputable clinics welcome questions about their fees, policies, facilities, staff, and services. Some even suggest that a woman use her pregnancy test as a trial run to see if a particular facility suits her tastes, needs, and pocketbook.

Choosing a clinic, of course, implies more than an attitude of consumerism; it also implies the presence of clinics to choose among. For city or suburban women this will present no problem. Every major metropolitan center and many smaller cities offer multiple possibilities; some "overbuilt" communities have even had discreet "price wars." The local yellow pages probably contain a heading for "Abortion" or "Abortion services," with several competing establishments advertising their services, hours, locations, the type of insurance and medicaid payments they accept, even the credit cards they honor.

But for women in small towns and rural areas feet rather than fingers often must do the walking. In the late 1970s, according to medical demographer Stanley Henshaw and associates, about 30 percent of those needing abortions couldn't get them, often because they couldn't locate or get to a convenient facility in time. Although the numbers of clinics are gradually increasing nationwide, Henshaw and associates noted in 1981 that "8 out of 10 U.S. counties have no facility in which legal abortions are performed, and only 5 percent of abortions are performed in nonmetropolitan counties, where 26 percent of women in need live."[5]

It's likely, of course, that many women who know everyone in their own small towns by name prefer to take a bus or car to the city for a "shopping trip," "job interview," or "matinee" rather than to walk into an abortion clinic on Main Street. Indeed, Warford has noticed this phenomenon even among city slickers; her clinic in Fairfax County, Virginia, a Washington, D.C., suburb, has a sister clinic in Montgomery County, Maryland, across the metropolitan area. Women from Falls Church or Alexandria, Virginia, often prefer to drive an extra half hour to somewhere they're less likely to know anyone, and so do their sisters from Silver Spring or Rockville, Maryland.

But this shouldn't obscure the very genuine obstacles that rural and small-town women often face in finding somewhere they can both get to and afford. Their tight communities may even constrain them from asking around among their friends. Particularly for them, therefore, the National Abortion Federation [NAF] toll-free hotline–(800–772–9100) in Washington, D.C., is a vital source. This nonprofit, professional organization can answer questions about procedures and suggest reputable clinics throughout the country. Local Planned Parenthood groups also provide reliable information about available resources. Commercial referral "services" and those offering advice on "problem pregnancies" are often merely fronts to channel women into certain enterprises or to dissuade them from abortion altogether.

Very knowledgeable advice is particularly vital for those past the twelfth week who want the D & E instead of a more dangerous, costly, and traumatic intra-amniotic procedure. Only a relative handful of physicians anywhere offer the D & E; whole states, indeed whole regions, may well have none. Texas, California, Colorado, and some East Coast cities probably account for the bulk of D & Es done in this country, but distance need not prevent a woman from obtaining one. Clinics charge so much less for the outpatient procedure than hospitals do for salines that even with the added expense of airfare to a distant city and a night in a hotel the D & E can make good sense on economic grounds alone. Although, as a general principle, women anticipating abortion should make their definite arrangements as early as practicable, the need for a D & E may constitute something of an exception. A day or two on the phone finding a qualified, well-recommended physician able to take the case can mean markedly less trauma, danger, and possibly even expense.

So, in practical terms, how should one proceed? The first step in arranging an abortion is getting reliable references. These may come from friends, friends of friends, the doctor or clinic that does the pregnancy test, the NAF hotline, or maybe even the phone book. If several acceptable alternatives exist, then personal considerations can help narrow down the choice. Is one location markedly more desirable than another, either in terms of convenience or anonymity? Does one facility offer a payment plan that particularly suits personal needs? Does one charge less? Does one have an atmosphere or decor that particularly appeals? Does a trusted friend strongly recommend one? In choosing among equally competent facilities, any of these considerations, or any similar ones that occur to the woman, are fully valid. As Zimmerman concluded, matters of atmosphere or ambience importantly affect the nature of the entire experience.

But how can one tell if a clinic is indeed competent and well run? Simply ask the person who answers the phone and see how closely the facility in question matches this description.

A competent clinic uses accepted medical procedures. This means the procedures used should closely resemble those explained in the previous chapter. There might be some slight variations, however, particularly in second-trimester methods. As Dr. Boyd points out, doctors develop particular preferences that work for them personally. Unnecessary changes in routine can cause unnecessary problems. Patients should understand what is happening and be permitted to express opinions on certain of the decisions to be made. But some decisions are strictly technical and strictly within the doctor's purview. It makes no sense to hire an expert and not take advantage of his or her expertise. Whether a patient has a pain medicine during dilation should be her decision; how often the laminaria should be changed is the doctor's.

Accepted medical procedures also include what happens before and after the procedure. The clinic should take a medical history, do a lab workup that tests the urine and blood, and after the procedure it should make provision to give a shot of Rh-immune globulin (often called Rho-Gam) to women who need it because they have the Rh-negative blood type. If these women become pregnant by men with the more common Rh-positive blood type, they can develop antibodies against an Rh-positive fetus; these can severely damage a later, wanted child. If received within three days of the abortion, the shot will prevent the formation of antibodies and safeguard later pregnancies.

Accepted medical procedures means, furthermore, that the tissue will be examined after it comes from the uterus and the woman will be promptly notified of any irregularity.

A competent clinic has an excellent safety record. This results from using practitioners very skilled in the particular procedures they perform. Nearly all states require that physicians perform abortions, but the handful that allow paramedics to do them can also offer excellent safety if the operator has constant practice and works under the direction of a knowledgeable doctor. The most desirable abortion practitioner is one who is constantly active doing successful abortions. The exact level of other training, prestige of qualifications, or board certification has little bearing on safety. As Dr. Boyd points out, the single most important factor in safety is the record of the particular person doing the procedure; this is especially true in the second trimester.

A competent clinic has good hospital backup. This means that a plan exists so that no more than a few minutes will elapse between a problem in the clinic and arrival at a well-staffed and well-equipped emergency room. It also means that transport will be by ambulance if necessary.

A competent clinic provides counseling and takes it seriously. This, indeed, is often cited as one of the great advantages of a clinic abortion over one in a hospital or doctor's office. The staffs of sizable clinics include trained, experienced counselors who will both help the woman review her decision and explain what she can expect. Counselors come from a variety of backgrounds; they may be nurses, lay women trained by the clinic, or have specialized graduate degrees. Those without professional training in general counseling techniques should have special instruction in recognizing women with problems serious enough to need the intervention of more expert colleagues. Counseling may take place either in small groups or privately. Both approaches have their strong proponents. Groups allow resources to go further and help keep costs down. They also provide many women with a bracing feeling of solidarity and companionship. Private counseling, however, allows for a franker exploration of personal feelings. Clinics that routinely provide group counseling should, however, offer private counseling to anyone requesting it. Women should also have the option of including the man or some other person in the counseling session. Some clinics also provide separate informational sessions for the people passing anxious hours in the waiting room. If, during the counseling session, a skilled counselor believes that the woman has not sufficiently resolved her feelings about the pregnancy to warrant an abortion at that time, then a reputable clinic will reschedule the procedure to give the woman more time to work her decision through.

A competent clinic will not perform an abortion that, in its professional opinion, appears inadvisable. This is vital for safety. Both emotional problems and a number of medical conditions may make an abortion inappropriate at a particular time or in a particular facility. Some medical problems need to be cleared up before an abortion can proceed; others require specialized monitoring equipment or personnel not available at the clinic. The clinic, however, should advise where and under what circumstances the abortion can proceed. A wise woman, therefore, gives a clinic a complete picture of her health history, especially if she has any illness, infection, or chronic condition; it makes sense to discuss any special problems with a clinic's medical advisor at the time the appointment is made. This will allow time for needed treatment or consultation with the woman's regular doctor.

A competent clinic provides follow-up. Two weeks after the abortion, if all goes well, a woman should have a checkup, either at the clinic itself or some other facility recommended by the clinic. At any time after the abortion, if all does not go well, the woman may need the attention of a doctor or counselor. The clinic should have a phone number that patients can call at any hour of any day to gain immediate information; it also should have a doctor on call at all times. In addition, a patient should have access to a counselor after the abortion in case of need.

A competent clinic is concerned about contraception. Many clinics provide birth control of all types, either at the time of the abortion or at the follow-up visit. If the clinic does not itself offer birth control, it should refer its clients to a facility that does.

A competent clinic has a pleasant atmosphere. This does not mean that it needs an elegant decor (which may add to expenses and thus to charges), but it must have a suitable recovery room where women can rest after their procedures, whether on beds, couches, or reclining chairs. This room also requires the constant supervision of a trained professional who can monitor such vital signs as pulse and blood pressure and immediately recognize any emergency.

A competent clinic respects its clients. This means that it treats both women and men as responsible individuals, regardless of their ages or the circumstances that bring them there. It may call patients by their first names in the interest of confidentiality, but in that case professionals should go by their first names too. It physically safeguards all records to ensure complete privacy; it should give out no information about patients on the telephone without their permission (even to confirm their presence). It should explain, both orally and in writing, what will happen. It obtains the patient's written consent to procedures. It should provide written instructions about special needs or restrictions during the days following the abortion. It should strive in every way to maintain its clients' dignity throughout their dealings with the clinic. Many clinics even ask women to fill out evaluation reports on their experience and to offer suggestions for improvement.

As generations of abusive illegal abortionists have amply demonstrated, the fact that a facility or practitioner offers abortion services does not guarantee that its patients are treated with dignity. A nurse-midwife recalls a grisly story told her by a client: During a D & E a doctor kept a sonograph screen where the patient could see it, permitting (indeed, compelling) her to watch the fetus come apart. He also told her, step by step, what he could feel through his instruments. This punitive, sadistic man was an accomplished surgeon; respect for patients depends not on skill but on outlook.

A competent clinic discusses its fees and charges frankly and openly. Many clinics charge a flat, all-inclusive fee for a first-trimester procedure, including birth control materials; the follow-up medical exam and counseling session, if desired; Rho-Gam; and whatever else may be necessary. Others charge separately for various services. The fee for a D & E will increase with the duration of the pregnancy. Whichever system a clinic follows, a woman should know in advance what her bill will be, when it is due, and what forms of payment the clinic will accept. Some clinics also can make arrangements for reduced or delayed payment in cases of genuine financial need. Some will process insurance forms and accept medicaid.

In areas that offer a number of alternative facilities, it's often worth a bit of effort to seek out one that both meets high professional standards and matches a woman's particular taste. Some people, for example, might like an informal, down-to-earth place with rock music playing in the waiting room (or even the procedure room) and staff members in casual street clothes. But to others these details might undermine confidence in professional skills; for them a more formal situation would be more reassuring. Her best friend's choice may not be a woman's own.

But details of style don't merit obsessive concern. Many styles of work can result in a positive experience. The most important consideration, beyond medical competence, is the establishment's attitude toward its work and its clients. It should respect the woman's decision and her right to make it for her own reasons, treat her with dignity, and allow her a feeling of control in all areas where that is possible. "No matter how difficult the decision was," Dr. Boyd says, "no matter how complicated the situation, I came to believe that it could be a positive life experience, and that out of this a woman could feel her strength, her control. The service could be provided in such a way that when it was over, a woman would feel good about herself, good about the people that provided the service, good about the experience." His Fairmount Center in Dallas, for example, strives to give women a feeling of autonomy, dignity, and confidence, and he finds that this helps in controlling anxiety, tension, and consequently even pain.

Anxiety is a far from trivial element of most abortion experiences. In her study of Philadelphia abortion veterans, Ellen Freeman found that the most trying period lay between confirming the pregnancy and obtaining the abortion. About a fifth of the women reported depression and a third reported anxiety during the days or weeks that the pregnancy was suspected but not diagnosed. But once they knew the truth, and before they could act on it, the incidence of depression and anxiety soared—just under half felt depressed and nearly 70 percent were anxious. By four months after the procedure, reports of depression and anxiety were way down to 13 and 14 percent, respectively.[6]

Although few women find the days of waiting, deciding, and arranging terribly pleasant, some suffer considerably more distress than others—enough, indeed, to affect the entire tenor of the experience. And here Beauvoir's and Zimmerman's insights prove most predictive. The deciding factor appears to be circumstance—specifically, the woman's place in her social world, the resources of help and understanding she can mobilize from those who care about her. The women who suffer most are those who receive the least—the least support, the least understanding, the least respect from those they love or who love them. Zimmerman's unaffiliated women, the ones without firm attachments and strong relationships, have the hardest time. From their study of abortion outcomes, Nancy Woods and Cynthia Luke conclude, "If distress exists, the major source is lack of support by partners."[7] Some other authors believe that this construes the situation too narrowly; plenty of women who never even told the man about the pregnancy appear to get through all right. But the central point is plainly valid. Support from someone, and preferably from those closest and most deeply involved, immeasurably eases the way. Psychologist Nancy Adler writes,

> The strongest negative reactions are likely to occur in women who do not themselves want to terminate their pregnancies but who were persuaded or coerced to do so by their partners or their parents. One source of stress on the woman is known or anticipated disapproval by significant others.[8]

In most cases, although an abortion happens physically to the woman alone, it and the pregnancy happen psychically to a couple. The man has a major role, for good or ill, in most abortion dramas, but to this day very little is systematically known about how he plays his part or what it means to him. Even more obstacles lie in the way of research on the men involved in abortions than obstruct the path to knowledge about the women. Researchers have very few ways of finding

them—quizzing people whiling away nervous hours in waiting rooms is a main sampling technique—and no way of assuring themselves of a representative sample. Men may refuse to own up to the situation, literally walk away from their
women, or simply not know. The men who idly turn the
pages of magazine after magazine on clinic couches obviously
represent the more supportive, more involved of those in
their situation.

But a further problem exists as well. Nearly the entire
attention of the abortion movement—and of the research it
has spawned—is centered on the woman, on her choice, her
psyche, her body, her self-image, her values, her rights. Almost no attention is given to the man on the periphery of the
action. In 1979 sociologist Arthur Shostak sought to review
the literature of male reactions to abortion, but, to his dismay, he found almost no literature to review. His own forth-
coming book will be the first full-scale study of the question.
In place of the vast stretches of library shelves overflowing
with sage words on abortion and the female psyche—those
literally hundreds of books and articles that have poured
from the pens of psychiatrists, physicians, journalists, and
polemicists—he uncovered a total of three studies on men
published since legalization. And of these the journalistic
component was high and the sample reliability low. Of his
own interviews with men, he writes,

> A sizeable minority of young males find their abortion
> experience more frustrating, trying, and emotionally
> costly than public and academic neglect of the subject
> suggest . . . [But though] a clear majority of the males
> thus far interviewed denied any serious emotional conse-
> quences, some in the minority group expressed a desire
> to have had more knowledge and a larger role in the
> abortion process."[9]

Whether it be the man in the case or someone else, a wise
woman equips herself with a helpful companion before she

sets out on abortion day; indeed, the facility may well advise her to bring someone along, if only because she may not feel quite well enough to drive or negotiate buses or subways by herself on the way home. She also goes with an empty stomach; a general anesthetic may become necessary at some time during the day, and it is best to be prepared. She should allow sufficient time—at least four hours—for her clinic stay and should not plan any strenuous activities for that day or the next. Although good clinics strive to give personal attention, the requirement to keep costs down usually prevents them from honoring personal schedules. Clinics that give group counseling schedule groups of women to arrive and undergo certain parts of the process together. People bothered by long stretches of idle waiting might want to bring something to occupy them—needlework or a book, perhaps.

Setting out may seem like the beginning of an espionage film—indeed, some of the secret signals, complicated directions, and aliases used before legalization would have done Hollywood proud; but the modern woman has no need to increase her susceptibility to pain by worrying. In the words of Dornblaser and Landy,

> Relaxation is the key. You are not going to a motel room. You are not meeting an abortionist in a warehouse. You are receiving a medical service, to which you are entitled, in a safe, welcoming environment staffed by competent, empathetic people—people just like yourself.[10]

Opening the door into the clinic may result in a bit of a shock. Up to now most women or couples have lived through their pregnancies essentially alone, usually striving for secrecy, often very isolated. She may have dealt with the clinic, and thus with the reality of abortion, only anonymously over the telephone. But at the clinic threshold it becomes public and concrete. On any day, and especially on Saturdays, a popular clinic's waiting room is full of people chatting, knitting, reading, or staring into space. The people come in all ages and both sexes: women from thirteen to forty-eight waiting for abortions; husbands, parents, boyfriends, and women friends covering an equally wide range. They come dressed in blue jeans and tailored suits; they bring their homework, their needlepoint, and their newspapers. "I didn't realize there would be so many others," many women say. Or, "I didn't realize there would be others like me. I thought I was the only woman of fourteen (or forty-three, or wearing a wedding ring, or nearing menopause, or playing varsity basketball) to do this." For many this sudden connection with a varied band of fellow beings all facing a similar crisis brings almost inexpressible cheer. In the muted bustle of the waiting room, among the dog-eared magazines and Danish-modern couches, the problem pregnancy can change from a solitary nightmare into a social fact; the woman carrying it can cease to be a lone deviant and become a member of a sizable—and respectable—class.

From the moment she gives her name to the receptionist, the woman becomes part of the clinic's efficient and well-practiced routine. Particular customs differ from place to place, but the same steps must occur regardless of their order.

- **She will make arrangements to pay her bill.** At clinics charging a flat fee this often happens first.

- **She will give the clinic information about herself.** This should include both her medical history and social situation.

- **She will learn about and consent to the procedure she is to undergo.** She might watch a film or filmstrip, read a brochure, or hear a formal or informal presentation. In particular, she will learn about the medical risks she faces and will better understand the unlikely but possible complications that may ensue. She then will give her formal written consent to permit the procedure.

- **She will give blood and urine samples for laboratory testing.**

- She will undergo a physical examination. This will include a pelvic exam, and which may embarrass some younger women unused to the gynecological table with its raised stirrups.

- She will learn about methods of contraception and choose one for herself if she wishes.

- She will meet with a counselor, either alone or in a group, to discuss her feelings and her decision.

- She will receive specific written instructions about how to care for herself in the coming weeks and how to recognize potential problems.

- She will undergo the abortion. In most cases the counselor or patient advocate will accompany her. Once the abortion is over, the emotion reported most often in all the studies is pure and simple relief.

- She will recover before leaving the clinic. For an hour or so she will rest under the constant supervision of a trained professional who monitors her vital signs, watches for any hint of trouble, and gives pain medication if needed. She will probably also receive light refreshment such as coffee, tea, bouillon, soft drinks, crackers, and cookies.

- She will receive a globulin shot if necessary.

This description of abortion day sounds very little like the confusing mumbo jumbo of many medical encounters. A well-run facility has as its primary goal to demystify the procedure, to prepare the woman psychically and physically to withstand it and learn from it. The unique history and nature of abortion has even spawned a special profession—one that is "unique in the sense that this discipline is not often represented in other areas of medical practice."[11] Although many women—and men—undergoing other traumatic medical procedures—hysterectomies, for example, or mastectomies, amputations, transplants, or cancer surgery generally—would benefit from discussions with a skilled, knowledgeable, supportive counselor, only abortion clients presently have this opportunity as a matter of routine. Society's preconception that abortion must be traumatic has made abortion's proponents work forcefully to assure that it generally is not.

The entire structure of a well-run clinic bends toward informing the woman of what she is doing and why. A wise woman takes advantage of the opportunity to ask as many questions as she needs or wishes to. "I know you may not want to think too deeply right now," said a wise doctor to a group of women soon to undergo abortions. "I know you may want to just skate on top of what's happening, but it's a good idea to clear up any questions while you have the chance."

A well-run abortion facility offers many opportunities and much encouragement to do just that. And in so doing it banishes the age-old terror of abortion day.

7/

THE AFTERMATH

"I know I made the right choice, so why do I feel so bad
about it sometimes?"

Woman quoted by Muhr

A woman sits, shortly before her planned abortion, talking
with a clinic counselor. The professional poses one of the
standard questions: "How do you think you're going to feel
after the abortion?" And then, write Carole Dornblaser and
Uta Landy, who have seen it happen many times, "all too
often a wary look comes over a woman's face, and she hesi-
tates to answer. There is a long pause, and she chooses her
words carefully. Finally she says, almost apologetically, 'I
think I'll probably feel fine.' "[1]

In what other medical situation does feeling fine make a
patient uneasy? When else does a person contemplating surgery suspect that she ought to regret not suffering more?
How often does a woman undergoing treatment need permission to hope for recovery? But, then, abortion is not like any
other medical procedure; indeed, it is not even mainly a medical procedure. If it were, there would be no books like this
one, and no profession of abortion counseling; libraries are
devoid of books on "Thinking About Tooth Extraction" and
hospital staffs innocent of the profession of tonsillectomy
counselor—procedures that match or outweigh a first-trimester procedure in purely medical risk; and even a D & E
hardly rates as major surgery. And yet, society expects—even

subtly demands—that abortion carry weighty consequences
for the women who dare to undergo it. So what can a woman
really expect in the days and weeks following an abortion?
How realistic is the hope of "feeling fine"?

In a purely physical sense, the odds are very good indeed.
As we have seen, first-trimester abortion is a very safe procedure, and even second-trimester procedures produce medical
problems only infrequently. Like all surgery, however—indeed, like crossing a busy street—abortion carries some risk
and requires of the patient a bit of caution and vigilance to
ensure that risks don't become realities.

Well-run medical facilities give surgical patients the special instructions they need in writing, and this goes for abortion clinics too. Before leaving, a woman should receive a
sheet telling her specifically what she should and should not
do, how to spot symptoms of trouble, and where to get help.
It also explains that some symptoms that may appear unusual
to the woman are merely normal signs of the body's return to
the nonpregnant state. A staff member should go over the
sheet with each woman, either individually or as part of a
group, to assure that she completely understands what to look
for and how to act.

Returning to the nonpregnant condition means essentially that the cervix and uterus contract to their previous size
and state and that the levels of hormones associated with
pregnancy drop down to where they stood before conception.
The healthy female body knows how to move effortlessly between states of pregnancy and nonpregnancy; in a sense,
that's what the female body is *for*, or at least why it is con-
structed the way it is. In her shrewd study of gynecology,
sociologist Barbara Katz Rothman observes that while a
man's body has only one "normal" state, women pass continuously through several: menstruation, nonmenstruation,
pregnancy, menopause. Every day the same sun rises and
sets; the moon, meanwhile, changes continuously, from night
to night. Is either more "normal?" And can any single state—
tiny crescent, growing quarter, or full, rounded face—fully

express or embody "moonness"? Modern medicine, taking changeless masculinity as its norm, has taught us to distrust bodily changes, to see them as signs of pathology or at least of danger. But any interruption of pregnancy—no matter what its cause—inherently implies a passage to the next phase of a cycle stretching over decades. Women who spontaneously miscarry experience essentially the same changes that follow abortion. What happens may seem "different"—especially to a woman with little or no prior experience of pregnancy—but if she has received decent medical care, these changes are almost always perfectly normal.

Three processes explain what a woman will feel and must do as she recovers from an abortion: The cervix will be open for a time and thus can't fully protect the uterus from bacteria in the vagina and beyond; the muscular uterus, meanwhile, is gradually clamping down to regular size and sloughing off any remaining bits of the special lining it built up to support the pregnancy; and the hormone levels are swinging much more rapidly than usual.

The open cervix means a genuine risk of serious infection. Some doctors prescribe an automatic course of antibiotic as a precautionary measure; others don't give medication without an established need. Taking the temperature twice a day for at least a week, however, will usually detect an infection in its early stages; anything above 100.4 degrees Farenheit demands immediate medical advice. Any cervical dilation, whether before or after abortion, demands the principle of care we've already noted: Nothing in the vagina, in this case for at least two weeks, and longer in the case of second-trimester procedures. This means no tampons; no douches; no suppositories (even if prescribed by a doctor for a minor vaginal infection discovered before the abortion); no swimming; and no vaginal sex of any kind. Tub bathing is more controversial; some doctors forbid it while others allow it. Personal taste and one's own doctor's advice should provide a guide here.

There's little beyond aspirin, heating pads, and waiting

that a woman ordinarily can or should do about the changes in the uterus per se. She'll probably feel cramps or other pain for a time after the abortion, and she may experience vaginal bleeding as well. Her job is to watch the progress of these symptoms. The cramps may last for several days, but they should decrease rather than increase and should never be more severe than those she felt during or immediately after the procedure. The bleeding should not exceed the amount of her normal periods, even though it may go on intermittently a good deal longer, sometimes up to three or four weeks. But under no circumstances will a woman making a normal recovery pass clots as big as a half dollar, soak more than one pad an hour, or need more than six napkins in a twenty-four-hour day.

A good recovery means running no fever and suffering only moderate cramps and bleeding. Anything else means trouble—and often serious trouble. The main dangers, in addition to infection, include: incomplete abortion, in which some tissue remains in the uterus; failed abortion, in which the pregnancy remains in the uterus; and ectopic pregnancy, in which the fetus has attached itself outside the uterus, whether in a fallopian tube, on an ovary, in the abdominal cavity, or elsewhere. This last possibility can spell sudden, mortal danger if the fetus becomes so large that it bursts the organ containing it. Such symptoms of pregnancy as morning sickness, tender breasts, or bloating should cease within days after the abortion. If they do not, it may mean that the pregnancy continues, unsuspected, either inside or outside the uterus. And any sudden, sharp abdominal pain merits *immediate* medical attention, preferably at a hospital equipped for emergency surgery.

Two to three weeks after the abortion, without fail, the woman needs an examination, either at the clinic or by another doctor. At that time she will be advised about the progress of her recovery and of any special steps she should take in the unlikely event of problems. Her period will normally begin about a month to six weeks after the abortion; if she began taking birth control pills right after the procedure, then it will come a few days after her first package is gone.

Physical recovery nearly always follows this simple and straightforward course. But what about the emotions, which have also played a vital part in the woman's experience? This answer often involves the third recovery factor we mentioned, namely, the hormones. The same process that stops the morning sickness, shrinks the swollen and tender breasts, and dries up any milk that may have formed can wreak changes just as great on a woman's state of mind. Although many women feel relief as their overriding, immediate, and lasting reaction, many also report "the blues," "the dumps," or "a funk" for the next few days. This usually isn't a serious depression but rather the same "down" feeling that plagues many women every month with their periods or right after they deliver a baby. And it comes from the same cause: Hormone swings often mean mood swings as well. But sadness, remorse, or depression beyond that, or lasting more than a few days, might signal more serious trouble in the woman's total adjustment to her pregnancy and her decision about it.

Just how common are real emotional problems? Can most women really expect to "feel fine" in an emotional sense too?

We can answer this question, in part, by asking another: Do women everywhere face this same worry? Cornelia Friedman, Rhoda Greenspan, and Fay Mittleman, psychologists who studied the consequences of abortion decisions, have observed

that there are many good, careful American studies of psychological sequelae [outcomes] of abortion, but there are very few in the Japanese, Russian, and East European literatures. There is high acceptance of abortion and little anticipation of specific psychological aftereffects in these countries.[2]

Few Japanese, Russian, or East European professionals probe the possible psychological outcomes because they already know the obvious answer: "I expect to feel fine." But for American women and the professionals who conscientiously see them through abortions, the question has genuine resonance. "We do . . . speculate," Friedman, Greenspan, and Mittleman continue, "that social values play a part in augmenting an individual's tendency toward guilt, grief, or self-punishment."[3] As we noted at the very outset, an abortion poses a question of meaning to an individual woman and in an individual life. That question of meaning frames the time of decision; it carries her through her abortion; and it stays with her afterward. A woman must decide, and decide, and decide again what her abortion means to her; and what she decides will determine how she feels about it and herself for undergoing it.

In cultures that do not view abortion as deviant; in countries where women who abort do not experience themselves as walking along—or perhaps even falling off—the very edge of acceptable womanly behavior; in societies where a decision to abort does not need an explicit moral defense because people recognize an implicit one in their understanding of femininity, women feel no need to apologize, no compulsion to defend or explain. Such societies provide women with an automatic rationale: They aborted because they wanted to and because abortion is their right—and is all right.

In American society, however, most women face a greater challenge. Abortion is all right in one sense—the law allows it—but, even so, it's less clear to many people that abortion is all right in any other sense. Almost 70 percent of Zimmerman's women disapproved of abortion to some degree before their own brush with it[4]; Freeman found similar feelings in Philadelphia. Mere weeks before she faced the sudden, unexpected need to find an abortionist, Fran, a philosophy student, wrote a term paper on Sartre's *The Age of Reason*, explaining why the heroine's planned—but unconsummated —abortion violated not only her own but every woman's fem-

ininity. Facing the same existential choice as the fictional character, but coming to a different—and easier—choice, Fran "had to confront abortion as a reality, not an abstraction. In that light, it's a whole different thing from what I had thought. It's not something that 'happens' to you; it's something you will yourself to do, and for your own reasons. Sartre didn't begin to express the agony of redefining yourself along lines you never expected to have to consider."

The abortion passage, in other words, has in large part to do with integrating this unacceptable, in some cases even unthinkable, act into one's personal history. How is a woman to accomplish this?

At one time—and not very long ago—the experts would have answered in unison, "Only at great psychological risk." The Jungian therapist Irene Claremont de Castillejo recalls:

> For years I have been much concerned at noticing the disturbances caused by past abortions upon the minds of my women patients. I had thought that this was due to the abortion itself, which I had assumed was contrary to woman's psychological makeup. But recently I have become overwhelmingly convinced that the bad and lasting effects upon a woman is not the fact of the abortion itself, but is artificially induced by [former] abortion laws. If my contention is correct that abortion has from time immemorial been part of women's lore, its possibility must be inherent in the deep layers of a woman's psyche.[5]

Perhaps Jill can't discourse as learnedly on the psyche, but she can vouch for her own experience. Her first abortion, during her college days in New York, was a haze of such harrowing anxiety, such indignity, such fear that her recovery took place mainly in the psychiatric ward at Bellevue. A later abortion—after legalization, her marriage, and a move to another city—didn't take her, in deep secret, to a solitary but skillful sadist who, amid constant demands for absolute silence, offered a shower of filthy epithets but no anesthetic as

he scraped out her womb; instead she went matter-of-factly to a rather bland clinic staffed by people almost annoying in their cheerful solicitude. Instead of seven hundred dollars in crumpled bills, she handed over the same credit card she uses at the druggist and the dry cleaner.

Another veteran of before-and-after recalls that before her first abortion in 1967, "I hid myself away for nearly a month, totally numb, full of fear," then slunk off to Mexico. "After returning, I dared not mention it to anyone. I felt very guilty, even though I know I had done the best thing for me." After her second abortion seven years later, in a clinic in her hometown, "I realized . . . that the big trauma I had gone through earlier had nothing to do with my own feelings about abortion but had everything to do with the feeling that I was by law a criminal for wanting control over my own life."[6]

But for decades no one—not women, not experts—arrived at this simple insight. Instead the women "hid themselves away, full of fear," and the experts extrapolated from what they knew, based on their caseloads and their psychological theories, never noticing that only women who had exceptionally severe reactions ever came for treatment. The others, the vastly more numerous women who coped on their own, never appear in the textbooks or journals.

American psychotherapy, throughout this century, and in all of its guises, has been basically Freudian. To his own classic question "What does a woman want?" Freud provided at least one answer: babies, or at least motherhood and the maternal role, to make up for the "deficit" of lacking a penis. If anatomy was destiny, then motherhood was not only a healthy woman's possibility but her ineluctable fate; if she could not fulfill it, she experienced sorrow. But if she *chose* not to fulfill it, indeed, if she consciously chose to destroy its imminent fulfillment, she did so out of deep, twisted hatreds, or weaknesses, or longings, and only at her own extreme peril. Sociologist Jessie Bernard, discussing the major older

psychiatric theories explaining what might motivate a
woman not to become a mother, concludes:

> The most important aspect of these several explanations
> is not the specific contents—neurotic over-strong pri-
> mary mother attachment or the dependencies or the nar-
> cissistic entitlements or the role ambivalence or the herd
> instinct—but the implication of deviance they imply. No
> one 'explains' the women who prefer non-motherhood as
> strong, autonomous women able to resist coercive pres-
> sures.[7]

A woman who wanted to terminate a pregnancy—any
woman, whether a fourteen-year-old rape victim or an impov-
erished forty-four-year-old widow with seven children to ed-
ucate—by definition suffered from significant maladjustment
that might well become even more severe were she allowed to
carry out her wish. The theory didn't differentiate between
not wanting a child now and not wanting one ever, between
desiring childlessness to preserve one's figure and to salvage
one's surgical residency, between not wanting any pregnancy
and not wanting this pregnancy. The theory made essentially
no distinctions at all.

And neither, equally significantly, did the law. The psychiatric explanations of women's desire to abort was really
little more than a justification for the state of the law. The
only women legally permitted to abort were those who could
convince a panel of doctors that they were just too mentally
ill to be mothers (or often even to endure pregnancy). How ill
this was, of course, psychiatry had no way of knowing. Of the
less than 1 percent of aborting women willing and able to
obtain legal procedures through psychiatric certification,
some undoubtedly were genuinely ill. Most, however, were
like Kitty, a smart, resourceful career woman in her late thirties who "paid the shrink and played the game" to get what
she had to have—and what she would have gotten by other

means had he refused. And he well might have, had she chosen him less astutely.

Well into the 1960s, Zimmerman observes, in the great majority of learned articles on the subject that instructed psychiatrists on how they should evaluate these cases,

> the conclusion was reached almost without exception that abortion inevitably causes trauma, posing a severe mental health threat to the woman involved. Research findings were presented along with the observation that completing an unwanted pregnancy was psychiatrically preferable to abortion in nearly every case, trauma posing a severe mental health threat to the woman involved.[8]

As late as 1973 a cunning study by Marsha Fingerer laid bare the psychological bias. She asked four groups—women seeking abortions, the persons accompanying them to the procedure, undergraduate psychology students, and postgraduate psychoanalytic students—to predict the feelings of women after abortion. The first two groups foresaw "only minor psychological discomfort," mainly brief depression. The psychoanalytic students, on the other hand, predicted much more serious depression. In the event, however, the abortion patients had actually overestimated their own psychological problems. "The psychological aftereffects of abortion seem to reside in psychoanalytic theory and societal myths," Fingerer concludes.[9]

But evidence contrary to prevailing views received stunningly little attention. A landmark study conducted in Sweden by M. Ekblad and published in the mid-1950s actually asked 479 recipients of legal abortions what they had in fact thought and felt. Of these women—all of whom passed Sweden's somewhat more lenient but still considerable psychiatric criteria and 58 percent of whom "had manifested symptoms of chronic neurosis" even before the pregnancy—fully 65 percent reported themselves "satisfied with their abortion and had no self-reproaches," 14 percent experienced a "mild degree of self-reproach," and only 11 percent regretted their action or "had serious degree of self-reproach."[10] And, as in many later studies on the subject, exactly what the women regretted was not made clear. Was it the abortion itself or the necessity to have the abortion? Did the women reproach themselves for terminating the pregnancy or for becoming pregnant under these circumstances in the first place? Did they regret this experience more, or differently, than they regretted a divorce, or losing a job, or an auto accident, or any other difficult or painful period in their lives? Like Ekblad, the researchers who followed in his wake did not bother to notice that their sample was severely skewed—ignoring as it did the 99 percent of aborters who could not or would not—whether through lack of time, money, or contacts, or an excess of self-respect—submit themselves for psychiatric permission.

No medical sleuth noted the existence of a medical phenomenon very much like Sherlock Holmes's celebrated "dog in the night-time." Holmes drew the perplexed witness's attention "to the curious incident of the dog in the night-time." "The dog did nothing in the night-time," the man protested. "That was the curious incident," Holmes replied.

From long experience doctors know that postpartum psychosis afflicts one or two new American mothers in every thousand severely enough to land them in hospitals for that reason alone; almost four thousand women a year nationwide. The well-known syndrome of postpartum psychosis forms part of every medical textbook's treatment of female psychology. But where, with half a million abortions annually in the years before legalization and over a million now, is the complementary syndrome of "postabortion psychosis"? Instead of the one to two thousand cases that "ought" to occur annually in this country—were abortion truly as great a psychic trauma as, say, childbirth—a psychotic state related specifically to abortion is, according to Potts, Diggory, and Peel, simply unknown.

Not until the years immediately preceding legalization, however, did these facts begin to penetrate the consciousness of researchers studying the psychology of abortion. But with surprising speed the new ideas sank deeply into that consciousness and brought it around 180 degrees. After a comprehensive "review of the diverse literature" on the subject, published in 1978, Henry P. David came to the

> conclusion that legal abortion does not carry a significant risk of psychological trauma, and that whatever psychological risks exists is less that that associated with carrying a pregnancy to term. Although the risk of psychological sequelae is greater in second trimester abortions [other than D & E], especially for the very young, who find it difficult to cope with delivering a recognizable fetus, sensitive counselling greatly reduces the momentary trauma. In those rare instances where post-abortion psychiatric disturbances appear, they are more likely to relate to the degree of adjustment existing before the pregnancy than to the abortion procedure. Feelings of guilt and depression, when noted, are usually mild and transient. It seems reasonable to conclude that for the vast majority of women abortion engenders a sense of relief and represents a maturing experience of successful coping and crisis resolution.[11]

The viewpoint of researchers—who had previously scoured results for the slightest hint of psychological trouble that they could possibly relate to abortion—swung around so drastically that for a time they seemed unable to make out any emotional ills at all in the blinding glare of their new certainty that most aborting women were—and remained—perfectly normal. This new enthusiasm is understandable, perhaps. Legalization permitted a much-desired new freedom and did, in fact, remove an important source of stress from the abortion passage. But the new research outlook may have been no more realistic than the one that preceded it. By reducing an abortion from a drastic gamble fraught with psychic danger to a minor incident meaning nothing more than "the moral equivalent of a nose job," psychologists after legalization reflected women's experiences no more accurately than they had before.

Indeed, counselor Marjorie Deutsch believes that to call abortion psychologically innocuous is no more realistic than calling it psychologically perilous. In her experience very few women pass through the experience without some regret, some feeling of loss or sadness. They often go through the well-recognized stages of mourning—anger, denial, bargaining—that precede a full acceptance of loss. Whether a woman mourns the child itself, her lost chance at motherhood, her lost image of herself as a wholly "good girl," or merely the anxiety and stress she suffered, she usually emerges with some sorrow, some regrets.

No more than any other loss does an abortion simply "go away." A woman's whole past life—whether good or bad—stays with her always. In a touching and controversial memoir published in the New York *Times* in May 1976, Linda Bird Francke introduced readers to her "ghost baby," which is all that now remains of her unwanted fourth pregnancy. But does this mean that she made a mistake in aborting? Does it mean that she deeply regrets her choice? "My own regret is the sheer irresponsibility on my part to become pregnant again. I pray to God that it will never happen again. But if it does, I will be equally thankful that the law provides women the dignity to choose whether to bring new life into the world or not."[12]

Francke tells her own story, and those of many women she spoke with, in a book whose title tersely describes her own feelings: *The Ambivalence of Abortion.* "The words 'You're pregnant' can never be received with indifference," she writes. "With those words, regardless of whether they provoke happiness or despair, a woman becomes instantly isolated in her individuality, in her health, in her present, and in her future. Her life is forever altered."[13] And whatever its outcome, the pregnancy will never completely leave her. Francke is—remains—deeply, but frankly, ambivalent. Barbara Radford agrees. "People get the impression that once you've made the decision, there's no ambivalence. That's not so. It's like any other large decision."

Abortion, however, is rarely treated "like any other large decision"; society tends to see it as a moral question or political controversy rather than the way aborting women see it, namely, as a regrettable but absolutely necessary practical step. In their zeal to prove that abortion did not do women overwhelming harm, proponents tended to argue that it hardly ever had any undesirable effects at all. In their zeal to show that abortion violates natural and human law, opponents have implied that any deleterious side effects necessarily outweigh all benefits. The limits of popular discussion thus don't allow for doubts and regrets of the kind that would be perfectly acceptable in some other sizable decision—to marry, for example, or take a job or buy a car. "My fiancé has some faults" or "I may miss my freedom somewhat" certainly don't argue persuasively against the institution of marriage, or even necessarily against a particular match. "I wish the job paid more" or "I had hoped to afford a new car instead of a used one" carry little weight in an otherwise necessary choice. And people permit themselves to recognize these drawbacks—these possibilities for regret—even after they have taken their vows or reported for work or made their down payment—in large part because the decisions themselves seem both legitimate and needed; few would argue that an absolutely perfect opportunity must present itself before it makes sense to work or drive—or even marry.

But abortion is different. Here people seem to demand a perfect decision—one without psychic cost. In the highly polarized climate of opinion surrounding abortion, and in the atmosphere of deviance, a woman may well feel that her decision must be entirely right or she will run the risk that it will prove entirely wrong. The two sides of the debate have appropriated nearly all the emotional ground for their ideological tug-of-war, so where can a woman grapple with her own sense of relief and her own feelings of regret? Hardly anywhere at all, observes Janice Muhr, in one of the most thorough studies available of the aftermath of abortion.

Most previous [postlegalization] investigators of the abortion experience have concluded that there is no apparent mourning period post-abortion. Such a conclusion is highly suspect, however, since the mourning process has been observed around events as simple as minor surgery. It appears to me that the experience of loss . . . after an abortion tends to get 'buried' for many women in the experience of guilt . . . Since the woman has voluntarily precipitated the loss, loss feelings, like guilt, generate uncertainty about the original decision.[14]

Feelings of sorrow and loss caught Sarah unprepared, for example, and left her tangled in guilt and vague remorse. "Mourning processes following losses consciously precipitated . . . tend to be blocked by guilt," Muhr believes, "such that the adjustment is characterized by a guilt-loss cycle which prevents resolution of feelings."[15] Sarah knows that her decision to abort was "right," and yet she can't get over a wish that her abortion had never happened, or that she hadn't gone ahead with it—or hadn't had to go ahead with it; she isn't sure exactly which. Of course, many people regret painful experiences, and wish they hadn't happened, without feeling guilty. Sarah's regrets, however, have a special twist; they seem to argue against her "right" decision and thus bring her constantly back to rethinking and defending her action. And because the decision caused her some moral qualms even as she made it, she must defend it strongly to argue down her own doubts. But it's difficult for her to mount a strong intellectual defense and, at the same time, regret what she's defending. Sarah might easily take a job that isn't perfect or buy a car that has faults, but she can't put her abortion into that category of necessary lesser evils; she wants it to be perfect so that she can stop defending it. Or, as the woman quoted at the head of this chapter asks plaintively, why should a good decision make her feel bad?

The problem, Muhr believes, lies not in Sarah's feelings but in the way society forces her to experience them. Society's "singleminded attention . . . to abortion as a moral issue [is] a major obstacle to the resolution of feelings" for the simple reason that "feelings of loss do not make sense within this construction except as evidence of wrongdoing." If a woman feels that sorrow follows a wrong choice, and she made that choice, then she cannot face and resolve that sorrow. She "focuses on managing her guilt, and mourning is inhibited."[16]

Inhibited mourning—an inability to acknowledge and resolve feelings of loss—can mean an inability to surround the experience and make it part of her own past, and thus to move beyond it. "For a long time it seemed as though someone else had done it," Fran says. "I couldn't decide what kind of a person would do such a thing, and so I didn't know what kind of a person I was." Fran suffered here, Muhr implies, from an inability to acknowledge, at the same time, both her regrets about her decision and its rightness.

> The way that abortion is construed socially implies that abortion cannot be both morally justifiable and a genuine loss, despite the fact that no such logical inconsistency exists . . . [There is] no social support of a mourning process post-abortion; those who favor abortion believe it shouldn't exist, and those who oppose it (perhaps) feel it is deserved.[17]

Thus, we see that the process of deciding does not necessarily end with the decision to make a clinic appointment, or even the decision to lie down on the surgical table. Rather, "for most, the issue [is] one of moral uncertainty—of struggling to define abortion as a proper act"—an act that "a person like me" could properly undertake, Zimmerman believes.

"In short, the abortion remained somewhat ambiguous and unsettled for the troubled women; for those untroubled, it was a closed issue."[18]

And yet, a year after their abortions "women consistently reported satisfaction with their choices," Smetana reports.[19] They must therefore have found some way to make sense of their apparently conflicting feelings, to work their decision into an acceptable picture of themselves.

But how? The best answer to date probably comes from Muhr. She interviewed 126 women—83 whites and 43 blacks—before their abortions at a freestanding clinic in Chicago. She interviewed 26 of them a second time, 3 to 4 months after their abortions, and she also found 13 other women who had undergone abortions 1 to 10 years earlier.

The women appear to face four crucial tasks in making sense of their experiences: "decision review," or evaluating the rightness of their own decision; "formulation of attitudes toward abortion in general," or an intellectual or moral framework for their action and others like it; "contraceptive behavior," or a strategy for avoiding similar problems in the future; and "ways of handling the fact of the abortion interpersonally, with male partners and with regard to social role."[20] A workable explanation of what abortion means, and therefore of what kind of person a woman must be to have one, demands an answer consistent with each of these four challenges. The way a woman meets them determines her ability to move beyond her abortion experience. And most women, Muhr believes, tend toward one of four distinct styles of adjustment, each involving an interlocking set of feelings, future actions, explanations of the past, and self-image, and each "characterized by the kind of conflict the woman acknowledges about the abortion and where she locates the control for the abortion decision."[21]

Sally, though not one of Muhr's subjects, might well typify the "status quo" style of adjustment, a resolution in which the woman asserts, and believes, that "I am as I was; the experience did not change me." A woman in her late thirties, she had almost finished her master's degree when she discovered her third pregnancy. With son and daughter about to enter high school, her thesis well under way, and her long, deadly years of caring for small children behind her, "I just couldn't stand the thought of another six years at home," she says. "The decision was easy." It proved so for her husband Ray, too; struggling to get his own business under way, he badly wanted the paycheck Sally could soon earn to give his new firm the breathing room it needed to grow. Neither of them saw any particular moral problem; neither, in fact, had attended church since childhood. Like Muhr's model status quo woman, Sally "identified no significant conflict about her plan of action . . . She . . . denies that there are any moral ramifications to her decision."[22] Furthermore, she "experienced [herself] as choosing *for* something as well as against the pregnancy," specifically her graduate degree and professional career. She also placed "significant energy into the option which has been chosen over the pregnancy,"[23] finishing her degree on schedule and soon thereafter finding a well-paying job in her chosen field. And, finally, she expresses "the most liberal views on abortion, emphasizing the right of any woman who wants one to have it, and the need for this to be a personal choice."[24]

Indeed, the only place where Sally departs at all from Muhr's description of the prototypic status quo woman is the degree of chagrin she felt at finding herself unwillingly pregnant. She and Ray pride themselves on their good sense, their clearheadedness, their ability to face and overcome obstacles. "I felt like a little fool," she says, "to make a mistake like that at my age." Even before she went for the abortion Sally and Ray decided to do away with the risk permanently. "Ray didn't want a vasectomy, so I had my tubes tied." But were it, through some unforeseen slipup, necessary to abort again, Sally, like her status-quo counterparts, would not hesitate. "The median attitude of this group is 'I would do the same thing under the same or similar circumstances.' "[25]

Were it necessary to have an abortion again, Fran would

come to the same decision as Sally—typical as the former is of Muhr's "I am more mature" style of adjustment—though she would find it a good deal more difficult. A woman like Fran, the philosophy student, Muhr writes, has "identified more dissonant feelings about the abortion decision than those who maintain a status-quo stance; [she] perceives [her] decision criteria as more complex."[26] To Fran, indeed, the abortion passage—deciding on, arranging for, and undergoing the abortion—remains, even years later, one of the pivotal experiences of her life. Although women adopt this approach because they feel conflict, they have "owned the abortion decision as a volitional one nonetheless"; it is theirs and no one else's because they willed it. Muhr continues:

> In the decision-making process, they have construed the pregnancy-abortion broadly enough to include negative levels of meaning in such a way that they do not threaten the validity of the choice. Post-abortion, they characteristically construe the difficult aspects of the experience as opportunities for learning, growth, and maturation.[27]

Fran, for example, sees this pregnancy as her first adult choice and her first occasion for adult independence and responsibility. For her it was almost an initiation into the darker aspects of her own personality, the "loss of innocence" so familiar from her literature classes.

But since people like Fran view abortion as so serious—perhaps because so painful—a step, their "attitude . . . toward abortion must allow for its being taken seriously,"[28] unlike Sally's, which takes it rather matter-of-factly.

> Women who experience themselves as more mature because of the experience expressed particular concern that women who undergo abortion do so 'responsibly.' Frequently, they commented on how distressed they were to observe many other women at the clinic who appeared to take the experience lightly. In formulating an attitude

toward abortion, they sought to distinguish themselves from 'those women.'[29]

Part of taking abortion seriously, for Fran and many others like her, means acting differently afterward. "To protect themselves, [they] demarcate their abortion as a learning experience. They cut themselves off from future negative implications by viewing themselves as having changed."[30] In Fran's case, first she turns her energies even more strongly toward the thing she opted *for*, namely, her studies. Second—although she would not use these words—she does " 'good works' intended to balance in some way the abortion act."[31] Specifically, she volunteers in abortion counseling and in the political movement to keep abortion legal. "The experience," she says, "politicized my thinking; I saw that abortion was not something I did because I was bad, but something that I had to do because of my position as a woman in this society." And, finally, she is a demon contraceptor now. If a first abortion made her responsible, then conscientiously avoiding a second one is proof of her newly won responsibility.

Responsibility has nothing to do with Judy's feelings toward her abortion; she has adopted the style that Muhr calls "I am a victim—adjustment as powerlessness." Like Fran, she permitted her boyfriend to talk her into intercourse despite inadequate contraception, but, unlike her, she allowed him to dominate her decision-making as well. She sat silently through the group-counseling session at her clinic. Only when the counselor pressed her to verbalize her feelings did she reluctantly say, "I don't want to do it, but I have no choice. There's no point talking about [the decision]." And, indeed, as a student living at home she has little practice in independent action. Afterward she has sought out people who will talk with her about her experience, but instead of analyzing her actions or exploring her feelings, she presses them for assurance that she did the right—indeed, the only possible—thing. The decision was as much her boyfriend's as hers. "Mike is with me in this," she told the counselor, "but he really felt we had to finish school. He can't possibly get married now, and we couldn't take care of a baby."

A woman who takes this approach—who refuses to "own" her decision—has "interpreted her abortion decision as a forced choice," Muhr says. "She feels coerced by circumstances or people into making her decision and perceives herself in a passive role with regard to her behavior and the feelings it generates in her."[32] Judy feels her conflict deeply— "I'm not sure abortion is right," she says—but she takes no responsibility for resolving it. Thus she can "avoid feelings of culpability . . . Her need to do this reflects her difficulty in developing moral arguments for abortion during the decision-making process. However, it also inhibits her use of any of the mechanisms for resolution available to women who 'own' their active role in their experience."[33] She hasn't, for example, made any effort to ally herself with other women who have aborted, to express any public opinion on the controversy, or, indeed, to change her life in any way.

Where Sally accepts her abortion as one of many proofs of her active adulthood, and Fran views hers as the threshold to a morally more challenging stage of life, Judy lets her abortion sink back into the haze of her own powerlessness. Her abortion does not connect to the other parts of her life history; it is merely something that "happened to her." And it may "happen" again; she allows prevention to lie beyond her control. Despite her counselor's repeated suggestions, she chose no effective birth control method after her abortion or at her checkup. "I'll have to think about it," she said. "I'll have to ask Mike." In this she only runs true to type, Muhr suggests.

If Judy can find some solace in helplessness, however, Patti can find none anywhere. She has adopted Muhr's fourth style, the "victim-persecutor," which "occurs among women who have been unable to rationalize their behavior from a moral perspective." Such women "can't disown responsibility (the victim) or view their 'mistake' as a learning experience (matured) or discount the significance of their guilt feelings (unchanged)."[34]

Unlike Sally and Fran, Patti believes that, though forced by social circumstance, her abortion was wrong; a Catholic upbringing, although partially rejected, taught her to believe this, and also that she is morally responsible for her actions. The new, liberal college world she now inhabited had not uprooted these deep, almost unconscious, beliefs; it had merely given her a liberal surface coloration. The fact that she had no money, that her boyfriend offered no support, that she couldn't turn to her family, that she was totally unprepared for motherhood—none of these excuse her for taking what she sees as "the easy way out," which, in fact, was for Patti almost unbearably difficult. Like Fran's abortion, Patti's was a true crisis, a turning point in her life. But, unlike Fran's, Patti's path turned downward, away from adulthood and autonomy. Within two months of the abortion Patti fell ill, was abandoned by her boyfriend, and impulsively moved to a new city where she knew no one. This bad choice led to others. The abortion had used up all her money, and she had left her job when she moved away from home. Friendless and almost penniless in an unfamiliar place, she took the only job immediately available, as a secretary at a university. She could scarcely have found work less suited to her temperament or her present predicament. The job paid poorly and also required a good deal of very exact record keeping; Patti, however, had not done secretarial work before and could barely pass the required typing test. The job also required her to keep detailed, very specialized files; in her distracted condition she constantly mislaid needed information. And, finally, it placed her among people she believed neither liked nor respected her. Within weeks she was circling downward into panic and despair, terrified she would lose the job she hated, and hating it and herself all the more because she needed it. She berated herself, saying, "I can't even hold on to this crummy job, even though it's way below my qualifications."

"In order to maintain her sense that she is taking responsibility," Muhr writes, a woman who has taken the victim-persecutor approach "extends her loss of faith in herself to other life situations, taking an attitude like, 'I am not allowed to trust myself' or 'after what I have done, I deserve little from life.'" This helps her to "maintain a role as ineffectual . . . The woman experiences herself as both victim and persecutor because, while the abortion has been a loss to her, her feelings of culpability lead her to feel that she deserves such suffering."[35]

Patti did not consciously link her woes to her abortion, but she spoke of it and her lost lover often, and with intense regret, and in utterly inappropriate situations, such as to co-workers and superiors she had known only a few weeks. At last, as her agitation grew until she no longer understood her predicament in any rational terms—a typing test or a work deadline loomed as grave, and personal, threats—a coworker said offhandedly, "Patti, I can't help you. You should see a psychiatrist." This banal suggestion struck Patti, who holds a graduate degree, as a stunning insight. Only years of therapy finally unwound the tangle of doubt and self-hatred that held her fast.

A response as tormented, as destructive as Patti's fortunately occurs only rarely; few women generalize their doubts and regrets into an indictment of their entire lives. But again we see—as we've seen in other cases—the powerful role played by the meaning a woman attaches to her experience. And this meaning is linked to—indeed, grows out of—the other meanings in her life. How she views herself as a person and a woman, what she believes about right and wrong, where she places responsibility for what happens to her—all shape her abortion into the particular pattern she sees. No one consciously chooses an adjustment style, just as no one consciously chooses a personality style. But honest attention to her own deep feelings, to the entire slant of her mind, can best guard a woman from making a serious mistake. We will never know whether Patti would have done better having her child and possibly giving it up for adoption; that choice bears its own deep distress. But the meaning she would have placed on that transgression, and the problems it would have brought her, might have taken a different form.

"You can't isolate the abortion from the rest of a woman's life," Barbara Radford insists. "I've never seen anyone who had an emotional difficulty following an abortion that wasn't trying to deal with something else." And, indeed, Patti had fled through a childhood darkened by a demanding but uncaring mother to emerge as a woman who lacked confidence in her own womanhood, her capacity to live as a worthy adult. She chose men who abused and degraded her; she dressed to hide rather than enhance a perfectly attractive figure in which she nonetheless saw serious flaws. Her decision to violate her own principles by aborting was merely one incident in a long history of mistrusting herself. Sally and Fran had the habit, or at least the inclination, of trusting themselves; their abortions made them stronger. Judy had the habit of trusting others, Patti the habit of trusting no one; their abortions made them weaker.

Muhr's and Zimmerman's women, and many, many others, all demonstrate that what determines the outcome is what the woman believes, in both her conscious mind and the realm of her dreams, that her behavior shows her about herself. This belief, of course, arises in part out of what she already believes about herself.

Perhaps the most poignant example of this truth comes from the saddest abortions of all, the genetic cases in which a couple decides to end a pregnancy that will, or might, produce a seriously defective child. "Selective abortion," write Bruce Blumberg, Mitchell Golbus, and Karl Hanson, "shakes the foundations of self-worth" because for most of us self-worth depends in part on our deep, unspoken faith in our "ability to create a normal, healthy family."[36] Even more terrifying, perhaps, than the thought of an unwanted child is the thought that the only child there can be is deformed, retarded, or will die young and painfully of some disease of the blood, the nerves, or the brain.

A couple who abort on genetic grounds are "innocent" in a way that other aborters are not. They do not violate society's norms about who should conceive. Nearly always married, nearly always wanting a child, they have, furthermore, taken the generous and responsible step of amniocentesis to assure the child's health. And yet in their own eyes they may carry a profound guilt, seeing themselves as tainted not merely by a single ill-considered action but in their very being. Beth, who aborted one pregnancy when it was inconvenient to have a child, had a much harder time aborting a second one when it was genetically necessary.

Families who know the disease from experience, however, like Dick and Ruth, who lost one child to Tay-Sachs, or Ken, who grew up with a severely retarded brother, have an easier time deciding and living with their decision. "I wouldn't put my family through that again for anything," Ken says. For him an abortion means not an opportunity lost but a terrible, lifelong sentence lifted.

And it's important to remember that any abortion can have profound meaning not only for the woman but for the man. We know less about men's reactions, of course, and they live under different social constraints than women. Deutsch observes, for example, that it's often easier for a young man's parents to stand behind a pregnant girl than it is for her own; in a surprisingly large number of cases it is his family she confides in and his family who accompanies her. From the man's point of view, of course, unplanned pregnancy comes under the heading of "boys will be boys" rather than "nice girls don't." Parents (especially fathers) may even take a secret pride in their son's "prowess" while outwardly bemoaning his carelessness.

But, still, for some men the overriding sense is loss—and very deep loss at that. Francke writes that her husband, who had argued strongly for the abortion, still mourned the son he might have had but now never will. And George responded to his girlfriend's abortion with sorrow and depression much more severe than her own. About a year before the pregnancy he had lost a leg in a motorcycle accident. Radford, who counseled him, suggests that the abortion might have triggered delayed mourning for that grievous loss and for his old life, as well as for the promise of new life now denied him.

By now, amid all these considerations of bad feelings and problematic adjustments, our original question has faded from view: Just how realistically can women "expect to feel fine" after an abortion? Despite all we've seen, a single conclusion remains. The great majority of women feel relief and continue to feel it; they would, in the same circumstances, do the same thing again; they walk away from it to lives often a good deal better, and certainly no worse, than those they had before. The great majority, in short, use an abortion experience "as a creative one, and one that builds ego strength."[37] Said one woman simply, "I made up my mind while I was lying there—I'm going to change my life. I quit my job, I broke up with my boyfriend. I'm moving in with my parents and going back to school. No drugs, no booze. Nothing! This time I'm not going to blow it."[38]

As she remembers her abortion, "it was nothing—it was over like that!" She snaps her fingers to demonstrate the ease. "Just in and out of that room in minutes!" But her own intentions show that she protests too much. For hardly anyone is an abortion "nothing." Only 15 percent of Freeman's women felt it was an "ordinary" experience; "nearly all . . . were distressed to some degree."[39]

But usually not to a great degree, or for very long. The great majority of women—emotionally healthy after as well as before abortions—appear to handle it as they do any other loss or trouble in their lives. From the perspective of four months, Freeman believes, "the most important factor in resolving the abortion experience is not absence of ambivalence or negative feelings but the ability to cope with those emotions."[40] This point bears repeating at the top of one's voice or in capital letters. She goes on:

Women who had not resolved their abortion experience four months later reported having attributes that suggested avoidance of feelings or negative self-image. Significantly more women who had resolved their feelings described attitudes that suggested a positive self-image, greater mastery and achievement, as well as a willingness to express and cope with feelings.[41]

Women who are normally resilient, who have the strength and openness to feel their emotions even when those emotions conflict, and to make their peace with ambivalence will come through this particular patch of trouble just fine.

A little help from their friends won't hurt either. Not all the experts agree with Freeman that resilience comes first. Many believe, with psychologist Esther Greenglass, that "the major factor that seems to be related to good psychological adjustment is the woman's perception that others close to her accept and support her emotionally."[42] These women see in the mirrors of their friends' faces that the abortion means no loss of worthiness or esteem. Women who have good social support—Zimmerman's "affiliated" women, for example—did consistently better, and had a consistently easier time, than those who didn't. Many of Patti's troubles, for example, go back to her feeling that no one loved or cared about her, or *could* love or care about so worthless a creature.

Social support means many things; it can be a single staunch friend or a whole network of kith and kin. Zimmerman, however, found something surprising and revealing: "Affiliated" women, those with strong relationships, tended to confide in fewer people than those without. The few they chose provided the strength they needed, and they were careful to preserve a flawless public image.

Social support might also take the form of a talk with someone who has gone through a similar experience, or even with a professional counselor. Many clinics offer follow-up counseling, since a number of counselors believe that women may need counseling more after the procedure than before;

talking it over with a good listener can greatly help in making sense of the experience. Marjorie Deutsch recalls the many women who had abortions long ago who have come to her for very short-term counseling, merely a session or two. "Many of them had never talked about it afterwards with anyone," she says. After Grace returned from her illegal abortion, for example, she told the one friend she had confided in, "Everything's okay," and then did not speak of it again for almost ten years.

Feeling fine is also more likely for women who know what to expect. As with the body's return to normal, the end of this emotional episode may entail some symptoms that seem a bit strange but that actually indicate a return to normal. Just as cramps can mean that the uterus is doing what it should, a sense of confusion or loss may be a very healthy sign. Such feelings, Marjorie Deutsch believes, are "part of a healing stage. You have to feel the sadness. You will eventually integrate." Or they may be part of something even bigger. As Marjory Skowronski has observed,

> Choosing an abortion is a major step toward self-determination and may elicit depression in women who previously did not make conscious choices and accept responsibility and the consequences of them. In this case, depression, then, is not a result of the abortion per se but a symptom of a larger growth cycle the woman has initiated.[43]

And in many cases this larger growth cycle means other changes, too, changes in self-regard, personal habits, and in relationships. The wise woman will analyze her use of contraception to see how she might improve it; the great majority of aborters were not using reliable, consistent contraception before their pregnancies. The great majority do so afterward.

But a woman may also notice or desire changes vis-à-vis the man involved. Four months later two out of three of Freeman's women still had the same boyfriend, lover, or husband. Almost half of Zimmerman's women reported their relationship unchanged or even improved. In a strong relationship, such as Suzanne and Doug's, their troubles had only made it stronger. "Doug really stood by me," Suzanne says. "We saw how much we really cared about one another." Three of Zimmerman's couples decided to marry.

But a crisis so intense throws a harsh, remorseless light on the secret, inner recesses of a relationship, making plain weaknesses that partners may have hidden or not even acknowledged. One in three of Freeman's women had left, or been left by, their men. More than half of Zimmerman's women saw their relationships deteriorate or collapse. In some cases, Muhr suggests, the man presents a handy target for the intense anger many women feel; the bonds between them often cannot bear this extra strain.

Other relationships may also look different in this unforgiving new glare. Some women break with siblings, friends, or parents who opposed their abortions. In all, almost half of Zimmerman's women reported "a disruption in at least 1 social relationship central to their lives."[44]

And so we can finally give a firm answer to our question: Can a woman reasonably expect to "feel fine" after an abortion? For a woman who has come to a decision that is right for her, even if it is not perfect; for a woman who has a realistic understanding that some bad feelings may follow; for a woman who is willing to treat herself gently during recovery; for a woman who has or can acquire sympathetic listeners and supporters, be they friends, relatives, or even a professional counselor or clergy member—the answer is a resounding yes.

8/

FINDING
THE MEANING

"It is at her first abortion that a woman begins to
'know.' "

Simone de Beauvoir

A wound that has healed no longer hurts when touched;
tougher, less sensitive tissue now covers the place that used to
smart and burn. Over time this new, but slightly different,
skin becomes "normal," so serviceable in everyday life that
we almost forget how we got it.

The memory of trouble, sorrow, or loss will, in a healthy
person, also become a "normal" memory, losing its ability to
stab when conversation or recollection touches it. The hurt
becomes the memory of pain rather than pain itself. An open
wound grows by itself into a smooth, shiny scar when healing
is allowed to take its own course. A painful experience can
heal into a different outlook on life.

For a woman whose trouble was an abortion, healing
means getting back a clear sense of what she's about and coming to some understanding of what she's been through. Making sense of her abortion in terms of her life and of her life in
terms of her abortion offers another benefit as well: Drawing
the right lessons from a mistake is the best way to avoid repeating it. But what is the lesson, and what was the mistake?

What, in Beauvoir's words, is it that a woman "begins to 'know'?" Says Fran,

> I hate to use words like 'radicalized' or 'having my consciousness raised'—they're so awkward and they wave so many flags. But, really, after my abortion I had to think about why it had happened, about why I had to go through such a trying time; I don't mean that I thought about the little facts—what happened on Thursday afternoon or Saturday morning. I mean that I had to think about the big 'why' of it. What was it about the kind of life I led that brought me to that point? And I realized that what led me to my abortion weren't only faults in myself but features of the whole way I had been taught to think about sex. And this led me to other thoughts about other things I had been taught and why I had been taught them. If this kind of thinking about myself and my place in life is radical, then I guess you can say my abortion radicalized me. At any rate, it changed the way I saw certain things.

Fran's, as well as every woman's, basic problem in dealing with abortion is to fit a new and probably unwelcome bit of data into what she already knows about herself and her world. For women like Sally, of course, it fits smoothly, without apparent strain; an abortion merely repairs faulty contraceptions. But for most women—Fran, Judy, Patti, and many others—an abortion is an experience unlike any other, and fitting it in may well squeeze parts of old ideas quite out of their former shapes.

The women Zimmerman studied tried two main strategies for fitting what nearly all of them saw as a piece of deviance into an acceptable self-image: Either they denied responsibility for the deviant act, saying "I had no choice" or "I was forced into it," or they denied that the act was deviant in the first place. For women taking the second, more daring, course, the simple idea that abortion is not necessarily wrong, unwomanly, or unjustified can lay bare a set of previously unsuspected connections between their pasts and the society around them. This inkling, this first glimmer of a notion that more might lie behind the event than personal failing, is a good part of what Beauvoir meant by "beginning to 'know.' " Fran asks herself:

> Why, after all, did I need an abortion? Because I became pregnant by a man I had no intention of marrying and at a time that I had no intention of being a mother. And why did I become pregnant? Because I wasn't using decent birth control. And why wasn't I using decent birth control? Because getting it meant going to a doctor or a clinic, and that meant admitting to myself and somebody else that I was sleeping with this guy and intended to continue doing so. And, after all, "nice" girls don't do that. That's why people like me get pregnant. Because we don't admit that we're 'that kind of woman'—the kind that sleeps with men—until it's already too late.

Fran's story echoes many others. Like her, the average American aborter is young, white, unmarried, of a middle-class background, somewhat ambitious about her future, childless, and pregnant for the first time. Fran's insight goes beyond the average, though. She has the ability to lift her own experience out of the merely personal and into the realm of a general condition; she has begun to see this event not as an isolated anecdote but as an illustration of a larger pattern of cause and effect. The great sociologist C. Wright Mills called this knack "the sociological imagination"; young radical feminists called it, much less elegantly, "having one's consciousness raised." But both meant seeing how individual lives intersect with the structures and values of society. What their abortions taught Beauvoir, and Fran, concerned the positon of women in society, what they did with that position, and how that position makes an act carried out under duress a million times a year by a representative cross-section of society into an act of deviance.

Why, indeed, do women become unwillingly pregnant? And how can they prevent it from happening again? On the simplest level, of course, Fran is right: They become pregnant because of inadequate contraception. The great majority of women seeking abortions either used no reliable method or used it improperly; in some other cases the method itself failed, as even the most dependable technologies will a small percentage of the time. Women who use properly the most reliable methods, however, have a very low rate of unplanned pregnancy; method failure can explain only a relative handful of the million American abortions a year. The rest simply didn't take advantage of available technology on the occasion when they conceived.

So a woman—really a girl—like Jenny should have had little cause for surprise.

I was fifteen when I started having sex with Jed. He doesn't like using rubbers. We sort of talked about me getting birth control, but I didn't really know how to do it. My mom just freaked out when I asked her, so I asked his mom and she said it wasn't her place. And we didn't have any money, and anyway, Jed said that if we watched the calendar or he pulled out, it would be okay. He's eighteen, and he's been around, so I figured he knew what he was talking about. Boy, was that a mistake.

But listen to this wife and mother—who had successfully controlled her fertility for years—recall a lovely summer evening on one of the rare weekends when her children were away. After a long, leisurely dinner mellow with the kind of unhurried, private talk they had rarely known since the babies arrived, her husband led her by the hand cross their back meadow to a wooded promontory overlooking a clear-running river. There the beauty of the sunset, the setting, and of each other overcame them. After years of conscientious fuss-

ing with gels and gadgets, she says, this one time there was
"no Delfen cream, no nothing. One night. But it was worth
it. It cost us three hundred dollars, but it was worth it."[1]

So the "simple" failure to use available contraceptive
technology may not be so simple after all. Writers and researchers, of course, have provided several explanations of
this interesting phenomenon. Most explain this seemingly irrational failure in psychological—usually Freudian—terms.
"In Freudian psychology, Leibnitzian philosophy, and
Calvinian theology," notes one psychologist, "accidents do
not happen"[2]; people do what they do because they have to,
because of who they are. A woman, for example, fails to contracept because of "immutable personal characteristics"[3]—a
low self-image, inadequate coping, bad family relationships in
her childhood, masochistic tendencies, a suppressed need for
mothering, or a desire for attention. Although she may not
know it, she actually wants her pregnancy, usually for reasons closely tied to her presumed psychological deficiencies.
She wants to punish herself, for example, or others; to realize
a fantasy or destroy one. Those who hold this view believe
that in order to prevent future pregnancies she must explore
her conflicts around the issues of sex and motherhood, acknowledge the irrationality of her former actions, and resolve
to act more constructively in the future.

But sociologist Kristin Luker rejects this explanation. Instead of *telling* women why they became pregnant, she decided to ask them. Specifically, she looked into what she calls
"the decision not to contracept." Sex without contraception,
she believes, usually doesn't result from unconscious compulsions; instead, it often represents a genuine decision, one
taken for reasons that, from the woman's point of view, constitute a sound, rational choice. Luker argues that no one can
understand unwanted pregnancy without looking at contraception from the woman's point of view.

The prevailing and 'outsider' position is that any pregnancy which is unwanted should have been prevented or

at least should have a history of attempts at prevention. If no attempts were made to prevent it, then the female (rarely does this analysis extend to the male half of the couple) is at best irrational and at worst pathological. There is an important but little-noted flaw in this reasoning. It assumes that women know at the outset what the eventual results of their contraceptive risk-taking will be: that over the long run 80% of all women exposed to intercourse without protection will become pregnant.[4]

Luker uses the term risk-taking advisedly. She believes that in failing to contracept, women are weighing, to the best of their knowledge, the advantages and disadvantages of unprotected intercourse, just as smokers weigh pleasure against the chance of lung cancer or skiers weigh excitement against the chance of broken bones. Skiers who end up in traction, however, are not considered irrational, just unlucky. Neither, indeed, are many smokers in cancer wards; so many others, after all, puff away a pack a day without obvious ill effects. After becoming pregnant, however,

women face the prevailing definition of the situation— that any pregnancy which is not actively prevented is irrational or inexplicable—and thus begin to feel that they must be either irrational or confused about what they really want . . . [But] their behavior leading up to the unwanted pregnancy is both reasonable and logical given *their* definition of the situation.[5]

But what definition of a woman's situation can make risking pregnancy preferable to using birth control? In the first place, of course, if a woman like Jenny vastly underestimates her chance of becoming pregnant, the risk may not appear very great. After all, Jed, who had "been around," assured her she had nothing to fear. And if a woman has taken similar risks in the past and gotten away with them, or if a doctor has idly observed that she may have trouble conceiving in the future, she may discount her genuine chances even further. But even if she accepts the danger at something near its real probability, taking the risk may still seem rational in certain situations. For the husband and wife on the riverbank, a moment's return to the spontaneity and freedom of their early love outweighed the emotional turmoil and strained budgets that followed. Running to the house for the foam, condom, and applicator might have saved them a good deal of trouble and money, but would have cost them something much more precious: that single, unforgettable night.

In the end, it's a question of weighing costs against benefits. Although an unwanted pregnancy can exact a high emotional and financial price, few women who've never been through one realize just how costly it can be. And it lies in the realm of the merely possible. The costs of reliable contraception, however, fall due immediately and aren't trivial either. Among the most onerous, Luker believes, are these:

> Contraception means acknowledging intercourse . . . Contraception means planning intercourse . . . Continuing contraception over time means that socially a woman is sexually available . . . Contraception means that sexual activity is planned and cannot be spontaneous.[6]

Over thirty years ago, in a wholly different social climate, two women and a handful of men made a fateful decision. Margaret Sanger and Katherine McCormick, both pioneering feminists, approached researchers trying to devise new methods of contraception and urged them to develop— quickly—a cheap, dependable mass form of birth control. In fact, they did much more than urge the doctors. McCormick, heiress to a great fortune, financially underwrote the project that resulted in the Pill, an idea that had, in turn, grown out of Sanger's struggles to help poor women control their sometimes suicidal fertility.

All agreed that the female reproductive system rather

than the male was the place to concentrate effort. This decision arose partly from considerations of physiology. Women's reproductive organs, they reasoned, being more numerous and more complex, offered more chances for successfully interrupting the chain of events leading to pregnancy. But other factors were at work, too. Women, perhaps because of their traditionally subordinate position in both sex and medicine, might feel less threatened by a doctor meddling with their innards. And most crucially, everyone's assumptions about sexuality led to the same conclusion. Since women bore the great social risks of pregnancy (and still do), women had a far stronger incentive, so these policymakers reasoned, to use contraceptives faithfully. Beyond that, Sanger's brand of feminism favored free love. A free woman for her was one who controlled her own body, one who, in Beauvoir's sense, "knew" herself as a sexual being.

Thus, while the older generation of mechanical contraceptives—the diaphragm, the condom, and foam—exacted costs from *both* sexes in terms of interrupted foreplay and loss of sensation, the newer generation of highly reliable physiological contraceptives—the Pill and the IUD—exact the costs in foresight, pain, and increased health risks entirely from the woman. Indeed, the costs for men—and their emotional investment in contraception—have fallen away to almost nothing.

In the days when the small birth control group was making its decision, however, it was a rare young man who went around without a pack of prophylactics hidden behind the cards and snapshots in his wallet. Getting a girl pregnant— "knocking her up," "getting her in trouble"—was very much the man's business, and much of the responsibility for preventing the accident and the trouble that would flow from it rested with him. If they slipped up, then he, if he were a gentleman and had any self-respect, would have to "do right by her": offer to marry her and mean it; or, if she wished, find her an abortionist, pay most or all of the costs, and see her through the ordeal. The predicament of the unlucky young couple was a staple not only of real life but of literature. *The Scarlet Letter*, for example, condemns Dimmesdale not only because he impregnated Hester Prynne out of wedlock but because he wouldn't own up. The fact that every sexual act with a "nice" girl that was not intended to end in pregnancy constituted, for a decent man, an open-ended commitment, gave him a powerful incentive to keep that condom handy and use it when the need arose. "A good girl deserved protection," one middle-aged man recalls, "and with a bad girl you wanted to protect *yourself.*"

But accidents happened—and with greater frequency in the days before virtually foolproof birth control. Condoms broke, especially when they were carried for months or years in the back pocket of an overly optimistic youth. Sometimes they interfered with his sensation to the point that he told her it wasn't "worth it" and there was nothing to fear. Sometimes things just "got out of hand," or he couldn't nerve himself to face the local druggist for refills. Sometimes she couldn't recall whether this day was "safe" or not; withdrawal takes more self-control than many men can muster, and even then it isn't very reliable. Lastly, condoms, and even diaphragms, simply fail a certain percentage of the time.

So when Sanger, McCormick, and the doctors made their decision to put contraception in the hands of women, it seemed a great, liberating idea. The decision certainly had the effect they intended. The person with the most to lose would control prevention; rates of unintended pregnancy were expected to plummet. But the decision had other effects they didn't intend—or even imagine.

When responsibility for contraception shifted to the woman, it shifted away from the man. And the practice of contraception, especially in illicit lovemaking, shifted away from that reasonably reliable but quite annoying male device, the condom, to the permanent, invisible female devices, the Pill or IUD. During the "sexual revolution" every woman—or so the mass media made it seem—was "on" something that in no way interfered with the spontaneity of the encounter or the pleasure of either party. And if she was not, she was so foolish, so "out of it" to perhaps "deserve" what might happen to her. A man could discharge his obligation with a perfunctory question about "precautions" or, if he moved in a relatively sophisticated circle, could assume that the question was unnecessary, perhaps even vaguely insulting.

The doctors—and the men—know that modern contraceptives, especially the Pill, work almost flawlessly in the laboratory and in clinical trials. One might therefore assume that they essentially solve the problem of unwanted pregnancy. But this idea hides another unwarranted assumption, a rather basic one about the nature of effectiveness. One study, for example concluded that the outer limit of effectiveness lies not in chemicals or contraptions but in "the interplay between contraceptive technology and various elements of human behavior."[7] No method is "effective" if people don't use it consistently and correctly. And many women who are supposed to "control" the modern contraceptives find them just too costly to use.

These costs take several forms, both physical and social. Rightly or wrongly, many women fear the Pill; it is known to increase the incidence of fatal blood clots, for example. Others dislike its side effects, which may include bloating, headaches, nausea, and depression. Some simply object to so rigid a daily regimen, and others to the idea of ingesting strong hormones every day of their lives. Although it has an excellent safety record for young women in good health, the Pill loses a good portion of its users in their first year. The IUD poses other problems: It can be painful—both to have inserted and to wear; it predisposes its wearers to potentially serious infections and perforations; and it can slip out and get lost.

Perhaps most serious of all, both of these very reliable methods require foresight on the part of the woman. She must obtain them in advance. In other words, she must plan to have sex. "Because it is not proper to do so," Zimmerman writes, "unmarried women do not generally think of themselves as sexually active persons." They do not "know" themselves in Beauvoir's sense. "They may engage in sexual activity, but that is viewed differently from being a sexually active person . . . Reliable methods of birth control suggest a *commitment* to sex.[8]

When a woman "goes on the Pill" for the first time, she does more than adopt a birth control method. She adopts a new identity as a person for whom sexual intercourse is a routine part of daily life. And as Fran pointed out, many find it difficult to admit to themselves or to men that they are "that kind of woman." As Luker observes, "If she is frankly expecting sex, as evidenced by her continued use of contraception, she need not be courted on the same terms as a woman whose sexual availability is more ambiguous. For many women the loss of this bargaining position outweighs all the benefits of contraception."[9]

In the romantic ideology that even many "liberated" women still unconsciously use to justify sex, intercourse is an act of love. A woman properly surrenders her virtue, or grants her favors, or makes the gift of her body only to an ardent, sincere, and persistent suitor who, by his very ardor, sincerity, and persistence wears down or vaults over the barrier of her maidenly modesty. He courts her, seduces her, and plies her with promises, gifts, and tokens of love. But a woman on the Pill needs no such courting; she obviously knows what to expect; there's little to mask the nakedness of the transaction. Divorced and widowed women know these assumptions all too well; the less gallant of their dates do nothing whatever to disguise the *quid pro quo* that they expect for an evening's entertainment.

But there remains one way for the experienced woman to salvage something of her pride. She can use an unreliable form of birth control. Not that she'll think of it that way—she'll see it as a contraceptive that "can be obtained more discreetly or in the case of 'withdrawal' and 'rhythm,' involve no device at all. These latter two involve no tangible evidence of sexual activity, no evidence of having planned sexual activity, and thus may be considered the least implicating to the self."[10]

Confirmation of Zimmerman's suspicion comes not only from the statements of women themselves but from the statistics on repeat abortions. Nearly 20 percent of the abortions done every year involve women who have aborted before. Despite the fact that a much higher percentage of repeaters than novices report using the reliable methods—and many of their abortions doubtlessly represent pure and simple method failure—large numbers of writers, researchers, and counselors worry a good deal about these women. Repeated abortions increase the chances of complications in future pregnancies; they expose women to the recurring risk of injury; and, many believe, they imply an unsatisfactory resolution of the previous abortion because they again involve contraceptive failure. Without denying that this may be so in a number of cases, it is still revealing to note that repeaters are likelier than novices to be widowed, divorced, or separated (although the majority of both groups are still single and never married).[11] Why should these experienced women, who during their marriages handled contraception with aplomb, suddenly start making the mistakes of young, naive girls? In some cases, of course, there was no mistake. The pregnancy was wanted at the time it was conceived, but the subsequent death or departure of the husband changed its meaning entirely. But in many others the husband was out of the picture long before the start of the pregnancy, or even of the relationship that caused it. When the husband left, these women, despite their years of respectable sexuality, ceased to defined themselves as "sexually active." They no longer lived with a man who had a right to assume they were always available—and often they could not foresee the possibility of finding another such man very soon. So they let their pills run out, had their IUD removed, or forgot to have their diaphragm refitted. And when another man did appear, they were unprepared, perhaps emotionally but certainly contraceptively.

This is hardly what Margaret Sanger had in mind. But,

then, she had in mind another sort of woman entirely, one who had long ago discarded—or perhaps never even possessed—notions of romantic purity. Her own turbulent life, often touched by the grim, complicated lives of the poor, had taught her, as Beauvoir put it, "to disdain bourgeois morality."

But many of the women who use the great technology Sanger foresaw have not yet become proud enough, self-confident enough, or realistic enough to take their futures and their sexuality in their own hands. Marjorie Deutsch wanted to find out why some young girls have repeat abortions and others do not. What most clearly differentiated her repeaters from the others was their low self-image—a lack of confidence and self-regard that Deutsch believes arises from poor family relationships. These girls simply thought too little of themselves to take the active steps necessary for their own protection.

Abortion, therefore, is often a "symptom of contradictory social expectations for women," Freeman concludes. "Social mores value self-management and individual choice in sexual bahavior, while paradoxically women's sexual activity is expected to be compliant and naive."[12] Modern women heard of "Sleeping Beauty" long before they read the "*Playboy* philosophy," and many, in spite of themselves, still wait for their prince to come and awaken their sexuality. Their mothers and grandmothers had a leaky but still operative code of chastity and honor to protect them from unwanted pregnancy; today's women have nothing but the Pill, and it only works if they use it.

In slang, even in demography, one refers to an unwanted pregnancy as an "accident." But, if so, it's an accident of a peculiar sort—rather like another type of "accident" we hear a great deal about. Every year around Labor Day and the Fourth of July the traffic authorities predict with macabre precision how many Americans will perish in auto wrecks during the holiday weekend. Strange that we can know in advance how many such "accidents" will happen! They certainly can't be aberrations, as the word accident suggests; that word is a smoke screen, a blind used to hide the true cause of the carnage. These wrecks—all those ruined lives—rather than being true happenstance, are rather like friction in the system, an integral, accepted, and expected part of how transportation works. Another kind of car, another sort of safety restraint, another type of roadway, another system of licensing and law enforcement could prevent nearly all of them. But society has made other choices. And because of the economics and sociology of the automobile, these "accidents" have to happen. The only thing "accidental" is whom they will happen to.

In just the same way, many pregnancies that end in abortion are friction in another system, an integral, expected part of the way sexual mores in this country work. And, indeed, a couple engaging in unprotected intercourse is more likely to run into trouble than any motorist on a busy interstate highway. "Looking back," Fran says, "It was almost inevitable that I would get caught. The only thing accidental was how long I got away with it."

Antiabortionists blame abortion on feminist ideas; women who abort, they say, reject traditional notions of womanhood. But research—and common sense—lead to just the opposite conclusion: It is "old-fashioned girls" who most often find themselves "in trouble." One study concluded that those who abort more often "accept traditional norms of sexual behavior in spite of their own sexual activity, and have a generally traditional view of women's roles."[13] The thoroughgoing feminist, the woman who unblinkingly accepts her sexual freedom and what it entails, has no qualms about protecting herself. "The use of contraception obviously demands that women feel at ease with themselves, their bodies, and their lovers, and also be able to accept the less romantic aspects of bodily functions."[14]

Luker seems, in fact, to be describing a man. Boys do learn—on the playing field, in the locker room, around the school yard—to see sex as an achievement separate from love and the body as a machine with certain less-than-ethereal aspects. Sex is something a boy expects to undertake; it is something a girl waits to have happen to her. Freeman's women told her that

> pregnancy happened to them: for some, because they 'wanted' to be pregnant (but later were forced to consider its appropriateness in terms of other objective conditions); for others, because they did not perceive themselves as instrumental in events in their lives. Their experiences had trained them to be receptive, to value themselves in terms of others' responses more than through their own contributions. They had no history of feeling that what they did made any difference, that their own actions and decisions had value to themselves and others.[15]

This hardly sounds like the stuff of rabid feminism, whose basic credo is that women must act independently and for their own reasons. But the need for approval—by their lovers—leads many women into intercourse, and their refusal to see themselves as legitimately sexual discourages them from taking proper precautions. At each decision point most women make what appears a rational choice. They do not start out contemplating abortions, or usually even becoming pregnant. Sociologist Patricia Steinhoff, who has investigated abortion among the various ethnic groups of Hawaii, makes an important distinction: "The question of why women desire abortion must not be confused with the issue of why they become pregnant, just as motivations for pregnancy must not be confused with motivations for having sexual intercourse."[16]

But if they have one set of attitudes going into the crisis, an unwanted pregnancy is for most women a true revelation: It reveals truths about their characters and lives in society that were previously hidden from them. As foxholes tend to make believers, abortions tend to make feminists; they give women, at the very least, new strength to accept and control their own sexuality—and perhaps even other aspects of their lives. This, at least, is how most observers interpret the tremendous swing to effective contraception by women who have aborted. They become capable of surmounting the social obstacles to getting and using contraceptives. And this new feeling that they can—and must—control their lives is the rest of what women "begin to know."

Knowing clearly what caused a mistake is the best way to avoid a repetition. A woman must understand the precise nature of the mistake she made: She took a bad risk. Chances are that she took it not because she was acting irrationally under the compulsion of destructive drives (although this does, of course, explain some cases) but because she was reasoning from bad premises and assigning faulty costs to the elements of her cost-benefit analysis.

Even counseling, Luker suggests, may not help. "There is a great deal of pressure . . . for women to admit that their risk-taking was irrational in the light of the subsequent pregnancy."[17] Perhaps it was, but that doesn't mean it appeared so beforehand. The medical establishment, she believes, has a vested interest in laying the blame on women rather than on the institutions producing and providing contraceptives that fail to meet many women's real needs. So a woman must hold fast to what she remembers of her own experience. Perhaps she discounted the possibility of an unplanned pregnancy out of simple ignorance or magical thinking. The point is not to ascribe guilt but rather to develop an approach that avoids problems in the future. If she intends to remain sexually active, then she must face her real contraceptive needs. So it's important for a woman to figure out exactly where she went wrong. Did she trust an unreliable form of birth control? Was she afraid to see a doctor? Did she simply refuse to acknowledge what she was doing? A blanket admission that "I was foolish" and a blanket determination to "be better" will prove no more effective than similarly vague and well-meaning New Year's resolutions. "At best," Luker argues, "counselling which offers psychologistic explanations of why a woman got pregnant simply fails to help her make a better and more rational decision next time. At worst, seeing a woman's behavior as irrational 'acting out' obscures the decisionmaking that is part of becoming pregnant and leaves her even less well prepared to think about taking risks next time."[18]

A woman operates not only in a psychic world of feelings and compulsions but in a concrete world of physical facts, one of which is the objective risk of conceiving from any given act of intercourse. To protect herself she has to understand that risk clearly, and a basic part of that understanding is giving costs their proper weight. Self-delusion ought to weigh very lightly against the risk of unwanted pregnancy.

Fran, for example, had previously felt that preserving her romantic illusion was "worth" the risk of unwanted pregnancy. She now knows that this assumption is false. "It appears that the more aware a woman is of the elements of her cost-benefit analysis, the less likely she is to make the same poor accounting twice in a row. The less aware she is, particularly of the latent functions of the pregnancy, the more likely she is to be a repeater."[19]

By "latent functions" Luker means the benefits of the pregnancy that the woman does not acknowledge. She raises an issue that verges on psychology, insisting that the woman know her own mind and desires. But, here again, as in their denial of sexuality, many women feel uncomfortable admitting and expressing strongly held wishes, especially when they concern other people. But pregnancy, which merely "happens" to her, might be capable of making other things happen too, things that she cannot imagine herself bringing about in any other way. Did she, for example, secretly think she could force her man into marriage? Did she wish to save a failing relationship? Did she seek her parents' attention or strive to win her independence from them? Did she want to prove her own fertility to herself? Did she expect that she might be able to raise a child alone? Any of these feelings would, of course, lower the apparent costs of pregnancy and make her far likelier to take risks. And any or all of these feelings could, if they continued unacknowledged, encourage her to take the same bad risk again.

But, as Shakespeare pointed out, we can "by indirections find directions out." Understanding the reasoning behind a bad decision can uncover desires otherwise hidden and suggest better ways of attaining them—if they can be attained at all. Finishing school and finding a job, for example, lead to a surer sort of independence than unwed motherhood and welfare. An abortion, properly understood, throws a searching light not only on a woman's attitude to her sexuality but on many other facets of her life as well.

So women who actively and effectively avoid pregnancy appear to hold some attitudes not shared by those who don't. Doesn't this undermine Luker's contention that there is no basic difference between women who don't become pregnant and those who do? Not necessarily; a given woman may well fall into either category at various times during the four decades or more of her reproductive life; she may even pass back and forth between them several times. Indeed, at least 80 percent of Luker's abortion subjects had at some time successfully contracepted[20]; some, like the wife on the riverbank, had done so for years on end. Some might have practiced meticulous birth control all their lives and merely have the bad luck to be extraordinarily fertile. There are a few women, for example, whose orgasms trigger ovulation; these "fertile Myrtles" are the bane of many technologies. One wife whose religion forbids artificial contraception and who has conscientiously watched her vaginal mucous and her basal temperature in an attempt to track her "safe" periods (a method, by the way, that works fairly effectively for many of those who practice it scrupulously), complained, "It's just awful. The number of kids we have is very close to the number of times we've had intercourse in the past few years. I just seem to get pregnant every single time. It's murder on a marriage."

So why, in the end, do most women become unwillingly pregnant? Because they have unprotected sexual intercourse. And why do they find themselves in that dangerous position? Because, depending on whom you ask, they're misinformed, unlucky, sinful, or self-destructive (or maybe several of the above). Because they lack self-knowledge, or self-reliance, or moral values, or ego strength. And what does all this say about them? Well, either that they're naive, or unenlightened, or sinful, or sick. But, as Shakespeare pointed out in another line from the same play, "There is nothing either good or bad, but thinking makes it so." It is the task of each woman who has undergone an abortion to decide which of these descriptions applies to her.

It sounds easy when put that way. For many women, though, choosing the right description can prove one of the most challenging tasks they have ever attempted. But, like all great challenges safely surmounted, it bears the possibility of very rich rewards. Dr. Boyd, who has seen many women struggle through this difficult time, believes that the experience can help them "feel their strength and control," something that happens all too rarely for most women in our society. And for many women this feeling lasts, and becomes part of a new, stronger, and more resilient self-image—part of a new, more self-reliant approach to life.

Beyond this the experience provides an opportunity—brutal perhaps, but effective—for what psychologists call "reality testing." It throws on many women's deepest—and perhaps least acknowledged—beliefs and relationships the harsh but healing light of truth. Comforting illusions, outgrown dependencies, and self-serving rationalizations have difficulty standing up to this unforgiving glare. Thus, a wise woman can use the opportunity to "know" a good deal that is new and useful about herself, her world, her relationships, her values, and her assumptions. And she can use this new under-

standing to build a life that more truly satisfies her own deepest desires.

To say this is not, of course, to recommend unplanned
pregnancy as a part of one's liberal education. Like many
other enlightening experiences—bone fractures and court lit-
igation, to name just two—it should be avoided at any reasonable cost. But neither need it any longer be a fearsome thing
for the woman who has the courage to face her own truth. In
that same great play about decision and illusion, Shakespeare
offers his own profound prescription for meeting trouble. Indeed, he summarizes the findings of all the researchers, writers, and polemicists on abortion in a single majestic line: "To
thine own self be true, And it must follow, as the night the
day, Thou canst not then be false to any [one.]"

NOTES

Chapter 1

1. Nathanson, 189.
2. Zimmerman, 101.
3. Ibid.
4. Potts, Diggory, and Peel, 544.
5. Zimmerman, 72.
6. Mohr, 254.
7. Gebhard et al., 196.
8. Ibid., 211.
9. Henshaw et al., 6.
10. Potts, Diggory, and Peel, 373.
11. Ibid., 534.
12. Beauvoir, 540.
13. Barr, 35.
14. Ibid., 98.
15. David, 85.

Chapter 2

1. Shereshefsky, Plotsky, and Lockman, 67.
2. Zajicek, 33.
3. Leifer, 20.
4. Freeman 1978, 152.
5. Steinhoff, 212.
6. Zimmerman, 40.

7. Leifer. 12.

8. Ibid., 13.

9. Ibid., 15.

10. Scott, 8.

11. Ibid.

12. Ibid., 9.

13. Zimmerman, 150.

14. Krucoff

15. Pearson, 482.

16. Rosen, 49.

17. Offerman-Zuckerberg, 171.

Chapter 3

1. Mohr, 262.

2. Ibid., 46.

3. Ibid., 165.

4. Ibid., 258.

5. Quoted in Kohn, 11.

6. Quoted in Potts, Diggory, and Peel, 276.

7. Feldman, 274.

8. Ibid., 286.

9. Ibid., 293–94.

10. Quoted in Hurst, 1.

11. Ibid., passim.

12. Ibid., 12.

13. Ibid., 13.

14. Quoted in Hurst, 19.

15. Bolton, 43.

16. Ibid., 45.

17. Ibid., 45.

18. Ibid., 42.

19. Ibid., 46.

20. Gustafson, 101.

21. Quoted in Nathanson, 265.

22. Sumner, 156.

23. Ibid., 152.

24. Ibid., 152.

25. Ibid., 151.

26. Ibid., 4.

27. Reiss, 280.

28. Allegeier et al., 278.

29. Ibid.

30. Quoted in Hurst, 11.

31. Ibid., 15.

32. Ibid., 3.

33. Gustafson, 104.

34. Callahan, 440.

35. Ibid., 425.

36. Harrison, 42.

37. Gustafson, 115.

38. Callahan, 496.

39. Ibid.

40. Ibid.

Chapter 4

1. "Doubts, Dilemmas," B3.

2. Zimmerman, 56.

3. Ibid., 56.

4. Ibid., 56.

5. Ibid., 56.

6. Ibid, 147.

7. Muhr, 125.

8. Gilligan, 19.

9. Ibid., 19.

10. Ibid., 100.

11. Smetana, 136.

12. Ibid, 82.

13. Freeman 1978, 152.

14. Zimmerman, 70.

15. Quoted in Sarvis and Rodman, 21.

16. Smetana, 29.

17. Ibid., 41.

18. Ibid., 50.

19. Ibid., 4.

20. Ibid., 82.

21. Ibid., 82.

22. Ibid., 70.

23. Gilligan, 100.

24. Smetana, 7.

25. Henry, 1.

26. Francke, 69.

27. Muhr, 107.

28. Ibid., 106.

29. Blumberg, Golbus, and Hanson, 800.

30. Zimmerman, 147.

31. David, 84.

Chapter 5

1. Potts, Diggory, and Peel, 188.

2. Ibid.

Chapter 6

1. Beauvoir, 546.
2. Zimmerman, 202.
3. Ibid., 163.
4. Potts, Diggory, and Peel, 194.
5. Henshaw, 6.
6. Freeman 1978, 152.
7. Woods and Luke, 223.
8. Adler 1979, 104.
9. Shostak, 574.
10. Dornblaser and Landy, 149.
11. Ibid., 143.

Chapter 7

1. Dornblaser and Landy, 161.
2. Friedman, Greenspan, and Mittleman, 49.
3. Ibid.
4. Zimmerman, 63.
5. Quoted in Skowronski.
6. Quoted in Skowronski, 106–7.
7. Bernard, 46.
8. Zimmerman, 22.
9. Fingerer, 224.
10. Quoted in Callahan, 67.
11. David, 97.
12. Francke, 20.
13. Ibid., 348.
14. Muhr, 179–80.
15. Ibid., 267.

3. Lauersen, 2.

4. Potts, Diggory, and Peel, 179.

5. Ibid., 238.

6. Ibid., 182.

7. Ibid., 182.

8. Ibid., 184.

9. Ibid., 190.

10. Ibid.

11. Dornblaser and Landy, 132.

12. Cates and Grimes, 405.

13. Potts, Diggory, and Peel, 204.

14. Ibid., 237.

15. Ibid., 203.

16. Stubblefield, 277.

17. Ibid.

18. Kaltreider, Goldsmith, and Margolis, 236.

19. Ibid., 236.

20. Ibid, 238.

21. Stubblefield, 293.

22. Hern and Corrigan, 7.

23. Quoted in Kaltreider, Goldsmith, and Margolis, 237.

24. Ibid., 238.

25. Stubblefield, 277.

26. Hern 1981, 417.

27. Dornblaser and Landy, 134.

28. Hodgson, 298.

29. Brenner and Edelman, 182.

30. Nathanson, 88.

31. Brenner and Edelman, 180.

32. Ibid.

16. Ibid., 229.

17. Ibid., 231.

18. Zimmerman, 185.

19. Smetana, 115.

20. Muhr, 184–5.

21. Ibid.

22. Ibid.

23. Ibid., 197.

24. Ibid., 185.

25. Ibid., 191.

26. Ibid., 201.

27. Ibid., 198.

28. Ibid., 201.

29. Ibid., 203.

30. Ibid., 203.

31. Ibid., 212.

32. Ibid., 213.

33. Ibid., 213.

34. Ibid., 218.

35. Ibid., 222.

36. Blumberg, Golbus, and Hanson, 806.

37. Luker, 76.

38. Quoted in Rosen, "Everybody," C2.

39. Freeman, 154.

40. Ibid., 153.

41. Ibid.

42. Greenglass, 99.

43. Skowronski, 111.

44. Zimmerman, 189.

Chapter 8

1. Luker, 51.
2. Maes, 18.
3. Luker, 16.
4. Ibid., 16.
5. Ibid., 42.
6. Ibid., 42.
7. Cobliner, Schulman, and Smith, 307.
8. Zimmerman, 85.
9. Luker, 49.
10. Zimmerman, 85.
11. Howe, Kaplan, and English, 1242.
12. Freeman 1977, 511.
13. Rosen and Martindale, 104.
14. Luker, 50.
15. Freeman, 510.
16. Steinhoff, 206.
17. Luker, 108.
18. Ibid., 146–47.
19. Ibid., 108.
20. Ibid., 89.

SOURCES

Adler, Nancy E. "Abortion: A Socio-Psychological Perspective." *Journal of Social Issues* 35:100–19 (1979).

———. "Sex Roles and Unwanted Pregnancy in Adolescent and Adult Women." *Professional Psychology* 12:56–66 (February 1981).

Aitken-Swan, Jean. "The Women's Story: Single Women." Pp. 130–65 in Gordon Horobin, ed., *Experience with Abortion: A Case Study of North-East Scotland.* Cambridge: Cambridge University Press, 1973.

Allegeier, A. R.; Allegeier, Elizabeth Rice; and Rywick, Thomas. "Orientations Toward Abortion: Guilt or Knowledge?" *Adolescence* 16:273–80 (1981).

Barr, Samuel J., and Abelow, Dan. *A Woman's Choice.* New York: Rawson-Wade, 1977.

Beauvoir, Simone de. *The Second Sex.* New York: Vintage Books, 1974.

Benditt, John. "Second Trimester Abortion in the United States." *Family Planning Perspectives* 11:358–61 (November/December 1979).

Bernard, Jessie. *The Future of Motherhood.* New York: Dial Press, 1974.

Blumberg, Bruce D.; Golbus, Mitchell S.; and Hanson, Karl H. "The Psychological Sequelae of Abortion Performed for a Genetic Indication." *American Journal of Obstetrics and Gynecology* 122:799–808 (August 1, 1975).

Bolton, Martha Brandt. "Responsible Women and Abortion Decisions." Pp. 39–51 in Onora O'Neill and William Ruddick, eds., *Having Children: Philosophical and Legal Reflections on Parenthood.* New York: Oxford University Press, 1979.

Bracken, Michael B.; Kerman, Lorraine; and Bracken, Maryann. "Abortion, Adoption, or Motherhood: An Empirical Study of

Decision-Making During Pregnancy." *American Journal of Obstetrics and Gynecology* 130:251–62 (February 1, 1978).

Brenner, William E., and Edelman, David A. "Menstrual Regulation: Risks and Abuses." Pp. 177–90 in Louis G. Keith et al., eds., *The Safety of Fertility Control.* New York: Springer-Verlag, 1980.

Burgwyn, Diana. "Childless by Choice." *Pennsylvania Gazette* 81, 1:24–29 (October 1982).

Callahan, Daniel. *Abortion: Law, Choice, and Morality.* New York: Macmillan, 1970.

Cates, Willard, Jr., and Grimes, David A. "Deaths from Second Trimester Abortion by Dilation and Evacuation: Causes, Prevention, and Facilities." *Obstetrics and Gynecology* 58:401–8 (1981).

———. "The Trimester Threshold for Pregnancy Termination." Pp. 41–51 in Marc J. N. C. Kierse et al., eds., *Second Trimester Pregnancy Termination.* Boerhaave Series for Postgraduate Medical Education, vol. 22. The Hague: Leiden University Press, 1982.

Cobliner, W. Godfrey; Schulman, Harold; and Smith, Vivian. "Patterns of Contraceptive Failures: The Role of Motivation Reexamined." *Journal of Biosocial Sciences* 7:307–18 (1975).

———. "Dynamics of Contraceptive Failures." *Journal of Psychology* 94:153–62 (1976).

Connell, Elizabeth. "The Risk of Being Female." Pp. 3–8 in Louis G. Keith et al., eds., *The Safety of Fertility Control.* New York, 1980.

Crabtree, Pamela Hinckley. "Personality Correlates of the Delayed Abortion Decision." Ph.D. dissertation, Adelphi University, 1980.

David, Henry P. "Psychosocial Studies of Abortion in the United States." Pp. 77–115 in Henry P. David et al., eds., *Abortion in Psychosocial Perspective: Trends in Trans-National Research.* New York: Springer-Verlag, 1978.

———, and Matejcek, Zdenek. "Children Born to Women Denied Abortion: An Update." *Family Planning Perspectives* 13:32–4 (January/February 1981).

David, Henry P.; Rasmussen, Niels Jr.; and Holst, Erik. "Postpartum and Postabortion Psychotic Reactions," *Family Planning Perspectives*, 13:88–92 (March/April 1982).

Deutsch, Marjorie B. Personality Factors, Self-Concept, and Family Variables Related to First Time and Repeat Abortion-Seeking Behavior in Adolescent Women." Ph.D. dissertation, American University, 1982.

Dornblaser, Carole, and Landy, Uta. *The Abortion Guide: A Handbook for Women and Men.* New York: Playboy Press, 1982.

"The Doubts, Dilemmas, and Hurts of the Abortion Business." Washington *Post,* September 12, 1982, p. B3.

Feldman, David M. *Marital Relations, Birth Control, and Abortion in Jewish Law.* New York: Schocken Books, 1974.

Fingerer, Marsha E. "Psychological Sequelae of Abortion: Anxiety and Depression." *Journal of Community Psychology* 1:221–25 (April 1973).

Francke, Linda Bird. *The Ambivalence of Abortion.* New York: Laurel/ Dell, 1982.

Freeman, Ellen. "Influence of Personality Factors on Abortion Experiences." *American Journal of Orthopsychiatry* 47:503–13 (July 1977).

————. "Abortion: Subjective Attitudes and Feelings." *Family Planning Perspectives* 10:150–55 (May/June 1978).

Friedman, Cornelia Morrison; Greenspan, Rhoda; and Mittleman, Fay. "The Decision-Making Process and the Outcome of Therapeutic Abortion." Pp. 38–44 in Roberta Kalmar, ed., *Abortion: The Emotional Implications.* Dubuque, Iowa: Kendall/Hunt, 1977.

Gebhard, Paul H.; Pomeroy, Wardell B.; Martin, Clyde E.; and Christenson, Cornelia V. *Pregnancy, Birth, and Abortion.* New York: Harper and Brothers, 1958.

Gilligan, Carol. *In a Different Voice: Psychological Theory and Women's Development.* Cambridge: Harvard University Press, 1982.

————, and Belenky, Mary Field. "A Naturalistic Study of Abortion Decisions." Pp. 69–90 in Robert L. Selman and Regina Yando, eds., *Clinical-Development Psychology.* New Directions for Child Development, no. 7. San Francisco: Jossey-Bass, 1980.

Greenglass, Esther R. *After Abortion*. Don Mills, Ontario: Longman Canada, 1976.

Grimes, David, and Hulka, Jaroslav F. "Midtrimester Dilation and Evacuation Abortion," *Southern Medical Journal* 73:44–51 (April 1980).

———; Hulka, Jaroslav; and McCutchen, Mary E. "Midtrimester Abortion by Dilation and Evacuation Versus Intra-amniotic instillation of Prostaglandin F2₂: A Randomized Clinical Trial." *American Journal of Obstetrics and Gynecology* 137:785–90 (August 1980).

———; Cates, Willard, Jr.; and Selik, Richard. "Abortion Facilities and the Risk of Death." *Family Planning Perspectives* 13:30–32 (January/February 1981).

Grobstein, Clifford. "When Does Life Begin?" *Science '82* 3:14 (March 1982).

Gustafson, James. "A Protestant Ethical Approach." Pp. 101–22 in John T. Noonan, ed., *The Morality of Abortion: Legal and Historical Perspectives*. Cambridge: Harvard University Press, 1970.

Harrison, Beverly Wildung. *Our Right to Choose: Toward a New Ethic of Abortion*. Boston: Beacon Press, 1983.

Henry, Neil. "The Best Thing." Washington *Post*, October 25, 1982, p. 1.

Henshaw, Stanley, et al. "Abortion in the United States." *Family Planning Perspectives* 13:6–18 (January/February 1981).

Hern, Warren M. "The Concept of Quality Care in Abortion Services." *Advances in Planned Parenthood*, vol. 13; rpt. in *Excerpta Medica*, 1978.

———. "Midtrimester Abortion." *Obstetrics and Gynecology Annual* 10:375–422 (1981).

———. "Outpatient Second-Trimester D & E Abortion Through 24 Menstrual Weeks Gestation." *Advances in Planned Parenthood*, vol. 16, rpt. in *Excerpta Medica*, 1981.

———, and Corrigan, Billie. "What About Us? Staff Reactions to D & E," *Advances in Planned Parenthood*, vol. 15; rpt. in *Excerpta Medica*, 1980.

Hodgson, Jane E. "Late Midtrimester Abortion." Pp. 297–308 in Jane E. Hodgson, ed., *Abortion and Sterilization: Medical and Social Aspects.* New York: Grune & Stratton, 1981.

Howe, Barbara; Kaplan, H. Roy; and English, Constance. "Repeat Abortions: Blaming the Victims." *American Journal of Public Health* 69:1242–46 (1979).

Hudis, Paula M., and Brazzell, Jan F. "Significant Others, Adult-Role Expectations, and the Resolutions of Teenage Pregnancies." Pp. 167–88 in Paul Ahmed, ed., *Pregnancy, Childbirth, and Parenthood.* New York: Elsevier, 1980.

Hurst, Jane. *The History of Abortion in the Catholic Church.* Abortion in Good Faith Series. Washington, D.C.: Catholics for a Free Choice, 1981.

Hymes, Kathleen. *An Ethical Inquiry: Where to Draw the Line.* Abortion in Good Faith Series. Washington, D.C.: Catholics for a Free Choice, 1981.

Induced Abortion: Guidelines for the Provision of Care and Services. WHO Offset Publication no. 49, Geneva: World Health Organization, 1979.

Kalmar, Roberta, ed. *Abortion: The Emotional Implications.* Dubuque, Iowa: Kendall/Hunt, 1977.

Kaltreider, Nancy. "Emotional Patterns Related to Delay in Decision to Seek Legal Abortion: A Pilot Study." *California Medicine* 118:23–27 (May 1973).

———; Goldsmith, Sadja; and Marogolis, Alan J. "The Impact of Midtrimester Abortion Techniques on Patients and Staff." *American Journal of Obstetrics and Gynecology* 135:235–38 (September 15, 1978).

Kierse, Marc J.N.C. et al. *Second Trimester Pregnancy Termination.* (Boerhaave Series for Postgraduate Medical Education, v. 22). The Hague: Leiden University Press, 1982.

Kohn, Richard. *The Church in a Democracy: Who Governs?* (Abortion in Good Faith Series), Washington, D.C.: Catholics for a Free Choice, 1981.

Krucoff, Carol. "Teens: Sex and the Parents' Right to Know," Washington *Post*, February 14, 1983, p. C5.

Kruk, Sue. "Pregnancy and the Single Woman." Pp. 147–76 in S. Wolkind and E. Zajicek, eds., *Pregnancy: A Psychological and Social Study.* New York: Grune & Stratton, 1981.

Lader, Lawrence. *Abortion II: Making the Revolution.* Boston: Beacon Press, 1973.

Lauersen, Neils H. *Investigation of Prostaglandins for Abortion.* Umea, Sweden: Nordic Association for Obstetrics and Gynecology, 1979.

Leifer, Myra. *Psychological Effects of Motherhood: A Study of First Pregnancy,* New York, Praeger, 1980.

Lewitt, Sarah. "D & E Midtrimester Abortion: A Medical Innovation." Mimeographed, 1981.

Liu, William T. "Abortion and the Social System." Pp. 137–58 in Edward Manier, William Liu, and David Solomon, eds., *Abortion: New Directions for Policy Studies.* Notre Dame, Indiana: University of Notre Dame Press, 1977.

Luker, Kristin. *Taking Chances: Abortion and the Decision Not to Contracept.* Berkeley: University of California Press, 1975.

Maes, John L. "The Psychological Antecedents and Consequences of Abortion." Pp. 17–23 in Roberta Kalmar, ed., *Abortion: The Emotional Implications.* Dubuque, Iowa: Kendall/Hunt, 1977.

Maine, Deborah. "Does Abortion Affect Later Pregnancies?" *Family Planning Perspectives* 11:98–101 (March/April 1979).

McLaughlin, Loretta. *The Pill, John Rock, and the Church,* Boston: Little, Brown, 1982.

Mohr, James. *Abortion in America: The Origins and Evolution of National Policy, 1800–1900.* New York: Oxford University Press, 1978.

Moseley, D. T.; Follingstad, D. R.; Harley, H.; and Heckel, R. V. "Psychological Facets that Predict Reaction to Abortion." *Journal of Clinical Psychology* 37:276–79 (April 1981).

Muhr, Janice. "Psychological Adjustment to First-Trimester Abortion." Ph.D. dissertation, Northwestern University, 1978.

Murphy, Cullen. "Watching the Russians." *The Atlantic Monthly* (February 1983), 33–52.

Nathanson, Bernard N., and Ostling, Richard N. *Aborting America.* Garden City, New York: Doubleday, 1979.

Offerman-Zuckerberg, Joan. "Psychological and Physical Warning Signals Regarding Pregnancy: Adaptations and Early Psychotherapeutic Intervention." Pp. 151–73 in Barbara Blum, ed., *Psychological Aspects of Pregnancy, Birthing, and Bonding.* New Directions in Psychotherapy, no. 6. New York: Human Sciences Press, 1980.

Olson, Lucy. "Social and Psychological Correlates of Pregnancy Resolution Among Adolescent Women: A Review." *American Journal of Orthopsychiatry* 50:432–45 (July 1980).

Ortof, Edna. "Psychological Aspects of Abortion." Pp. 56–66 in Barbara Blum, ed., *Psychological Aspects of Pregnancy, Birthing, and Bonding.* New Directions in Psychotherapy, no. 6. New York: Human Sciences Press, 1980.

Osofsky, Joy D.; Osofsky, Howard J.; and Rajan, Regna. "The Psychological Effects of Abortion: With Emphasis Upon Immediate Reactions and Follow-up." Pp. 188–205 in Howard J. Osofsky and Joy D. Osofsky, eds., *The Abortion Experience: Psychological and Medical Impact.* New York: Harper & Row, 1973.

Pearson, J. F. "Social and Psychological Aspects of Extra-Marital First Conceptions." *Journal of Biosocial Sciences* 7:453–96 (1973).

Potts, Malcolm; Diggory, Peter; and Peel, John. *Abortion.* New York: Cambridge University Press, 1977.

Ramsey, Paul. "Reference Points in Deciding About Abortion." Pp. 60–100 in John T. Noonan, ed., *The Morality of Abortion: Legal and Historical Perspectives.* Cambridge: Harvard University Press, 1970.

Reiss, Ira L. "Some Observations on Ideology and Sexuality in America." *Journal of Marriage and the Family* 43:271–83 (May 1981).

Rooks, Judith Bourne, and Cates, Willard, Jr. "Emotional Impact of D & E Versus Instillation." *Family Planning Perspectives* 9:276–77 (November/December 1977).

Rosen, Norma. "Everybody Wants to Do Something About Baby-Making," New York *Times,* December 2, 1982, p. C2.

————. *At the Center.* Boston: Houghton Mifflin, 1982.

Rosen, Rae Hudson. "Adolescent Pregnancy Decision-Making: Are Parents Important?" *Adolescence* 15:43–54 (Spring 1980).

————, and Martindale, Lois J. "Abortion as 'Deviance': Traditional Female Roles vs. the Feminist Perspective." *Social Psychiatry* 15:103–8 (April 1980).

Rothman, Barbara Katz. *In Labor: Women and Power in the Birthplace.* New York: Norton, 1982.

Sarvis, Betty, and Rodman, Hyman. *The Abortion Controversy.* 2nd ed. New York: Columbia University Press, 1974.

Schulman, Harold. "Biologic Obstacles to Abortion." Pp. 2–7 in Gerald Zatuchni et al., eds., *Pregnancy Termination: Procedures, Safety, and New Developments.* Hagerstown, Maryland: Harper & Row, 1979.

Scott, Lucy. "Intentionally Childless and Delaying Women: Psychosocial and Psychosexual Factors." Paper presented at the American Psychological Association, August, 1981.

Shereshefsky, Pauline; Plotsky, Harold; and Lockman, Robert F. "Pregnancy Adaptation." Pp. 67–102 in *Psychological Aspects of a First Pregnancy and Early Postnatal Adaptation,* New York: Raven Press, 1973.

Shodell, Michael. "The Prostaglandin Connection." *Science '83* (February 1983), 78–82.

Shostak, Arthur B. "Abortion as Fatherhood Lost: Problems and Reforms." *The Family Coordinator* 28:569–74 (October 1979).

Silber, Tomas. "Abortion in Adolescence: The Ethical Dimension." *Adolescence* 15:461–74 (Summer 1980).

————. "Values Relating to Abortion as Expressed by the Inner City Adolescent Girl—Report of a Physician's Experience," *Adolescence* 15:182–89 (Spring 1980).

Skowronski, Marjory. *Abortion and Alternatives.* Millbrae, Calif.: Les Femmes Press, 1977.

Smetana, Judith G. *Concepts of Self and Morality: Women's Reasoning About Abortion.* New York: Praeger, 1982.

Smith, E. Dorsey. "Abortion." Pp. 90–105 in E. Dorsey Smith, ed., *Women's Health Care*. New York: Appleton-Century-Crofts, 1981.

———. *Abortion: Health Care Perspectives*, Norwalk, Conn.: Appleton-Century-Crofts, 1982/

Steinhoff, Patricia G. "Background Characteristics of Abortion Patients." Pp. 206–31 in Howard J. Osofsky and Joy D. Osofsky, eds., *The Abortion Experience: Psychological and Medical Impact*. New York: Harper & Row, 1973.

Stubblefield, P. G. "Midtrimester Abortion by Curettage Procedures: An Overview." Pp. 277–96 in Jane E. Hodgson, ed., *Abortion and Sterilization: Medical and Social Aspects*. New York: Grune & Stratton, 1982.

———, et al. "A Randomized Study of 12mm and 15.9mm Cannulas in Midtrimester Abortion by Laminaria and Vacuum Curettage," *Fertility and Sterility* 29:512–17 (May 1978).

Sumner, L. W. *Abortion and Moral Theory*. Princeton: Princeton University Press, 1981.

Williams, George Huntston. "The Sacred Condominium." Pp. 146–71 in John T. Noonan, ed., *The Morality of Abortion: Legal and Historical Perspectives*. Cambridge: Harvard University Press, 1970.

Woods, Nancy Fugate, and Luke, Cynthia. "Sexuality and Abortion." Pp. 215–35 in Nancy Woods Fugate, ed., *Human Sexuality in Health and Illness*. 2nd ed., St. Louis: Mosby, 1979.

Zajicek, E. "The Experience of Being Pregnant." Pp. 31–56 in S. Wolkind and E. Zajicek, eds., *Pregnancy: A Psychological and Social Study*. New York: Grune & Stratton, 1981.

Zimmerman, Mary K. *Passage Through Abortion: The Personal and Social Reality of Women's Experiences*. Praeger Special Studies Series. New York: Praeger, 1977.

INDEX